International Research on Poverty Reduction

This book series covers poverty reduction practices and experience, knowledge mobilization, poverty reduction strategy analysis, and comparative research of different poverty reduction models. By analyzing China's poverty reduction approaches and experiences, and comparing them with those of other countries, this book series provides policy makers, researchers and practitioners in poverty reduction with theoretical and technical support, as well asproviding a new channel for sharing experiences as well as facilitating collaboration and communication in poverty reduction development fields between China and the rest of the world. Poverty remains a crucial development issue for the world, and China has become an important player in the global endeavor in poverty reduction and development. China has made a substantial contribution to the achievement of the Millennium Development Goals (MDGs) by reducing half of its poverty population.

More information about this series at http://www.springer.com/series/11685

Changsheng Zuo · Chengwei Huang ·
Xiaojun He · Xiaolin Wang
Editors

Inclusive Development and Poverty Reduction

SSAP

Springer

Editors
Changsheng Zuo
The State Council Leading Group Office
of Poverty Alleviation and Development
Beijing, China

Chengwei Huang
China Poverty Alleviation
and Development Center
Beijing, China

Xiaojun He
International Poverty Reduction
Center in China
Beijing, China

Xiaolin Wang
Institute for Six-sector Economy
Fudan University
Shangai, China

Translated by
Fang Li
Beijing, China

Xu Chen
Beijing, China

ISSN 2195-9781 ISSN 2195-979X (electronic)
International Research on Poverty Reduction
ISBN 978-981-15-8445-9 ISBN 978-981-15-8446-6 (eBook)
https://doi.org/10.1007/978-981-15-8446-6

Jointly published with Social Sciences Academic Press
The print edition is not for sale in China Mainland. Customers from China Mainland please order the print book from: Social Sciences Academic Press.

This Springer imprint is published by the registered company Springer Nature Singapore Pte Ltd.
The registered company address is: 152 Beach Road, #21-01/04 Gateway East, Singapore 189721, Singapore

Editors' Note

From 2007 to 2011, we successfully organized five annual meetings of the Global Poverty Reduction and Development Forum. They were attended by thousands of officials from developing countries working in government agencies responsible for poverty reduction and social development, experts and scholars, and representatives of international development agencies, non-governmental organizations and the private sector. The forum provided an opportunity for participants to share successful poverty reduction experiences of developing countries, allowing them to strengthen communication and cooperation in this area and to deepen mutual understanding and friendship. A formal decision has now been passed that, to mark the International Day for the Eradication of Poverty, the annual meeting of the forum would from now on take place on October 17.

Following extensive discussions, "inclusive development and poverty reduction" was chosen to be the theme of the 6th annual meeting of the Global Poverty Reduction and Development Forum. This background report features contributions solicited from noted experts and scholars.

I have many people to thank for bringing this project to fruition. They are Prof. John Taylor, Dr. Huang Chengwei, researcher Su Ming, Prof. Li Shi, researcher Cai Fang, Dr. Wang Meiyan, researcher Jia Jingdun, and researcher Zhu Lizhi, as well as those who reviewed the reports, including Christophe Bahuet, Assistant Country Director of the UNDP China, Hou Xin'an, Deputy Country Director of the UNDP China and Project Officials Pei Hongye and Zhang Yan, and Dr. Zhang Deliang, Dr. Li Linyi, Dr. Liu Qianqian, Dr. Liang Yi and Project Officials Ms. Zhou Liang and Ms. Gao Rui of the IPRCC.

Editors' Note

Contents

Chapter 1
Inequality in Middle-Income Countries: Analysis and Suggestions

John Taylor

1.1 Main Issues

1.1.1 Issue 1: Most of the World's Poor Come from Middle-Income Countries

Most of the world's poor are found in the middle-income countries, instead of low-income countries. Whichever way we measure it, according to the per capita income standard or the multi-dimensional poverty index (MPI), the result is the same,[1] and has already been confirmed by the latest poverty estimates.[2] These show that, if based on a poverty line of USD1.25 per day, 74% of the world's poverty-stricken population live in middle-income countries; and, if based on the poverty line of USD2 per day, 79% of such people live in middle-income countries. If the poverty line is set at USD2 per day in the middle-income countries, 35% of the world's poor come from India, 16% from the People's Republic of China, and 28% can be found in Nigeria, Indonesia and Pakistan. In contrast, less than 25% of the world's poor live in low-income countries. This trend will continue when predicting the data up to 2015 (Tables 1.1 and 1.2).[3]

Although many countries have gained much wealth and thus have become middle-income countries (or have climbed up to the rank of upper-middle income countries from being lower middle-income ones), many of them still have serious poverty

J. Taylor (✉)
London South Bank University, London, UK
e-mail: johngtaylor@hotmail.com

[1]These indexes together constitute the multi-dimensional poverty index (MPI), which is listed in detail in the *Human Development Report* published by the UNDP in 2010 and 2011.

[2]These poverty estimates can be found in the 2012 Povcal data. See the 2012 data published by the World Bank Development Data Group on the Povcalnet website.

[3]Please refer to Chandy and Geertz (2011).

C. Zuo et al. (eds.), *Inclusive Development and Poverty Reduction*,
International Research on Poverty Reduction,
https://doi.org/10.1007/978-981-15-8446-6_1

Table 1.1 Prediction of Global Poverty Distribution and Incidence Based on the Poverty Line of USD1.25 per day and USD2 per day, 2008

	Poverty line of $1.25 per day			Poverty line of $2 per day		
	Population (million)	As a percentage of global poor population	Incidence of poverty (percentage of population)	Population (million)	As a percentage of global poor population	Incidence of poverty (percentage of population)
East Asia and the Pacific	265.4	21.5	14.3	614.3	26.1	33.2
Eastern Europe and Central Asia	2.1	0.2	0.5	9.9	0.4	2.4
Latin America and the Caribbean	35.3	2.9	6.9	67.4	2.9	13.1
Middle East and North Africa	8.5	0.7	2.7	43.8	1.9	13.9
South Asia	546.5	44.3	36.0	1,074.7	45.6	70.9
Africa south of the Sahara	376.0	30.5	47.5	547.5	23.2	69.2
Low-income countries	316.7	25.7	48.5	486.3	20.6	74.4
Middle-income countries	917.1	74.3	19.5	1,871.1	79.4	39.7
New middle-income countries (after 2000)	651.7	52.8	33.4	1,266.4	53.7	64.9
Lower-middle income countries	711.6	57.7	30.2	1,394.5	59.2	59.1
Excluding lower- middle income countries including India	285.6	23.1	23.4	569.4	24.2	46.7
Upper-Middle income countries	205.5	16.7	8.7	476.6	20.2	20.3
China and India	599.0	48.6	24.3	1,219.5	51.7	53.8
PINCIs	785.9	63.7	26.1	1,570.0	66.6	52.2
Fragile states (OECD)	398.9	32.3	39.9	665.4	28.2	66.6

(continued)

Table 1.1 (continued)

	Poverty line of $1.25 per day			Poverty line of $2 per day		
	Population (million)	As a percentage of global poor population	Incidence of poverty (percentage of population)	Population (million)	As a percentage of global poor population	Incidence of poverty (percentage of population)
Total	1,233.8	100.0	22.8	2,357.5	100.0	43.6

Note Povcal adjusts the base year using linear interpolation method. PINICs refers to Pakistan, India, Nigeria, China and Indonesia. Fragile States refer to 45 OECD member countries (2011), taken from *Divided We Stand: Why Inequality Keeps Rising*, OECD Paris. *Source* This table comes from Sumner (2012). [Data in the table has been processed by Povcal (2012)]

problem. It is the fact that solving the poverty problem of middle-income countries has become a national issue to be vigorously addressed, because these countries are no longer eligible for international assistance after achieving certain development.[4]

1.1.2 Issue 2: Inequality Is Increasing in Many Middle-Income Countries

Inequality is a serious problem in many middle-income countries, and, moreover, the problem is going from bad to worse.[5] In per capita terms, inequality in most middle-income countries is more serious than that of OECD members, and, in most cases, inequality is growing. This is mainly concentrated in some middle-income countries in the Asian region, as shown in the Table 1.3.[6]

Apart from measuring inequality through per capita income data, there is a wealth of evidence to show that middle-income countries have persistent inequalities in other areas, most conspicuously in education (measured by the net enrolment ratio of the wealthiest 1/5 of the population) and health (measured by the infant mortality rate of the wealthiest 1/5 of the population).[7]

---

[4]This conclusion poses a challenge for development assistance. For example, what policies should be implemented to best solve this problem: there are more poor people in eight Indian States than in twenty-six African countries in Sub-Saharan Africa.

[5]For example, in the upper-middle income countries, the Gini coefficient of South Africa is very high, reaching 63.1, while it is 54.7 in Brazil and 55.9 in Colombia; in the lower-middle income countries, the Gini coefficient of Angola is 58.6 and 56.3 in Bolivia. These data come from the World Bank's *World Development Indicators 2012*.

[6]Data come from the Asian Development Bank (ADB) (2012, p. 47).

[7]For details, please refer to ADB (2012, p. 47) and OECD (2011, pp. 56–57).

Table 1.2 Twelve Countries with the Highest Number and Proportion of the Poverty-Stricken People in 2008, Based on the Poverty Lines of USD1.25 and USD2 per Day (Countries that started moving from low to middle income in 1990 are in the gray rows)

	Percentage of the world's poor ($1.25 per day)	Percentage of the world's poor ($2 per day)	Country classification (based on calendar year data)		GDP per capita per day (PPP is based on 2005 USD)	
	2008	2008	1990	2009	1990	2009
1. India	34.5	35.0	Low-income country	Lower middle-income countries	3.4	8.2
2. China	14.0	16.7	Low-income country	Upper-middle income country	3.0	17.0
3. Nigeria	8.1	5.4	Low-income country	Lower-middle-income country	3.9	5.6
4. Bangladesh	6.0	5.3	Low-income country	Low-income country	2.0	3.9
5. Democratic Republic of the Congo	4.5	2.6	Low-income country	Low-income country	1.7	0.8
6. Indonesia	4.2	5.2	Low-income country	Lower- middle income country	5.5	10.1
7. Pakistan	2.3	5.2	Low-income country	Lower- middle income country	4.4	6.5
8. Tanzania	1.4	1.6	Low-income country	Low-income country	2.4	3.4
9. Philippines	1.3	1.6	Lower-middle income country	Lower- middle income country	7.0	9.2
10. Kenya	1.2	1.1	Low-income country	Low-income country	3.9	3.9
11. Vietnam	1.1	1.6	Low-income country	Lower- middle income country	2.5	7.5
12. Uganda	1.1	0.9	Low-income country	Low-income country	1.5	3.1

Source Taken from Sumner (2012). The data in this table have been processed by Povcal (2012) and *World Development Indicators 2012*

Table 1.3 Gini coefficient of selected middle-income Countries

Country	First year	Final year	Gini coefficient: 1990s	Gini coefficient: first 10 years of the 21st century
China	1998	2008	32.4	43.4
India	1993	2010	32.5	37.0
Indonesia	1990	2011	29.2	38.9

1.1.3 Issue 3: Inequality May Hinder Development

One of the reasons is that continuous inequality may exert a negative impact on economic growth. In the past, a certain degree of inequality was seen as conducive to stimulating investment and growth. In recent years, however, it has also been found that continuous inequality in middle-income countries has had a negative impact on growth, as it will lead to the improper distribution of human capital, unsustainable forms of production and consumption, and instability of greater risks. More evidence becoming available points up to the fact that long-term economic growth and more equal income distribution are strongly linked, indicating that, in the long run, sustainability and the reduction of inequality may have a strong mutual promotion effect.[8]

The second reason is that the worsening inequality in recent years is an important factor fueling the international financial crisis, which has brought macroeconomic instability to middle-income countries.[9]

The third reason is that existing inequality will weaken the overall poverty reduction efforts. At a given growth rate, the more serious the inequality, the smaller are the results of poverty reduction work. Let's look at the official poverty line of the Chinese Government. From 1981 to 2001, if inequality in rural areas does not increase at the same rate as national growth, the number of the poor living under the official poverty line in China would be less than 1/4 of the current actual number—in other words, the poverty rate in 2001 should be 1.5%, rather than 8%.[10]

The fourth reason is that persistent inequality may lead middle-income countries into the so-called "middle-income trap".[11] Many middle-income countries in the 1960s were still at the same level in 2008. Only thirteen managed to escape the "middle-income trap" and were able to become high-income countries in 2008. To a large extent, these countries had been relying on export-oriented growth strategies, resulting in inequality in income distribution and asset distribution, while the government continued to follow a counter-productive policy leading to continuation of this inequality. The continuation of this distribution mode, together with these policies, hindered development of the domestic market and held down the overall growth of residents' consumption. The latter aspect, however, is the basis for sustainable growth.

As inequality will have a potential impact on growth fundamentals, financial stability, poverty reduction and sustainability, middle-income countries see it as an important aspect of their policy development, and have increasingly become aware of just how important it is.

[8]For details, please refer to Berg and Zettelmeyer (2008), Berg and Ostry (2011).

[9]With regard to this problem, please see Stiglitz (2010); and also see Stiglitz (2012).

[10]Please refer to Ravallion and Chen (2004).

[11]For details, see Gill and Kharas (2007).

1.2 Why Inequality Persists in Middle-Income Countries

There exist serious inequalities in middle-income countries, and the situation is still deteriorating. What are the main reasons behind this?

One of the main reasons is the regional impact of economic development, which is particularly uneven in middle-income countries. In those regions with strategic, locational or infrastructural advantages, the accumulation of development benefits remains higher than in other regions, resulting in the change of income distribution in spatial terms. At the same time, some social or moral vulnerable groups, mainly in some backward regions, experience an exacerbation in this inequality.[12] From a macro perspective, this situation prevails in the urban-rural income gap and regional income gap, and the regional income gap of middle-income countries has been expanding in the past ten years.[13] China and India are good examples. The income gap between urban and rural areas and regions of the two countries has widened considerably.[14] During the same period, the inequality in Indonesia and Vietnam was also largely due to the same type of income gaps. In the period from 2002 to 2007, the income gap between cities in the Eastern and Western China widened by 25%. If the overall inequality is viewed by combining the regional inequality with the urban-rural inequality, the results show that China, Vietnam and India have high inequality, reaching 53, 36 and 32%, respectively.[15] In recent years, Brazil has been the only middle-income country where the urban-rural gap has not expanded, because, in the mid-1990s, the average per capita income in rural areas grew faster than that in urban areas.

A major factor contributing to regional inequality is the continuing difference in educational opportunities, leading to an overall income gap in middle-income countries. Although the primary school enrollment rate in middle-income countries is close to that in high-income countries, there is a large gap in the enrollment rate among different groups and different regions. Generally speaking, the primary school enrollment rate in rural areas is lower than that in urban areas, and girls are still more vulnerable in this regard. This trend is more obvious in the middle school stage. Take the primary school enrollment rate in Pakistan in 2008 as an example. The rate for the richest twenty percent of the population there was twice that of the poorest one-fifth. The difference rises to five times in the secondary school in terms of net enrolment ratio and twenty-seven times in higher education. The Asian Development Bank (ADB) recently conducted a survey of eight selected middle-income countries in the region, finding that at least twenty percent of income inequality is caused

[12]For a detailed discussion of this "concentration" phenomenon and regional weakness in the early 21st century, see World Bank (2006).

[13]For information on widening gap, see OECD (2011, chapter three, pp. 53–55).

[14]For detailed information about China, see Li and Luo (2011).

[15]See ADB (2012, p. 70).

by education inequality.[16] In the period from 1995 to 2007,[17] of all middle-income countries in Asia, inequality was caused mainly by the gap of national education level. China's data rose sharply, from 8.1 to 26.5%.

The widening income inequality may also be related to the development of technology. Advanced technology needs skilled labor that receives higher wages than that paid to technologically weak workers, thereby contributing to a widening gap of the income distribution. The same period also saw constantly widening income gap between regular employees and contract workers. In recent years, the growth rate of income inequality in middle-income countries has increased significantly: the income of China's richest 1/10 of the population is five to six times that of its poorest 1/10, while that in India is twelve times (double compared with the 1990s), and that in South Africa is twenty-six times.[18]

While income inequality exists, the proportion of labor income has, since the early 1990s, been greatly reduced compared with capital income, which is the same in all middle-income countries in this period.[19] One (more obvious) reason is that technological innovation in some middle-income countries has led to increased productivity (so capital has a higher return than labor); however, it is also because the financial crisis in 2008 produced differing effects for different economic groups. It is also because of the current popular "rent-seeking" behavior[20] supported by governments that have introduced policies to reduce taxes on finance, capital gains and profits, a move that makes it possible for some rich people to get more benefits than they deserve. For example, in China, inequalities in recent years have been driven by the great export growth after 2001, and the large increase in exports has enabled a lot of profits to flow into creating speculative property bubbles. As China rarely restricts capital flows in these areas, this process has become very easy.

The average level has improved overall, but there are still significant inequalities in access to health facilities in middle-income countries. This is best reflected in the infant mortality rate and urban-rural mortality rate of each 1/5 of the population by wealth. In all middle-income countries in Asia, the mortality rate of the poorest fifth and of the rural population is higher than that of other groups.[21] Access to health facilities remains unequal. For example, a recent (2008) assessment showed that 57.9% of the surveyed population in eleven provinces of China failed to receive medical treatment due to economic difficulties.[22] Similarly, a 2009 survey of poverty-stricken villages revealed that 43.8% of the families had sunk back into poverty due to

[16]The countries selected for the survey include China, India, Indonesia, Pakistan, Vietnam, the Philippines, Bhutan and Thailand. See *WB World Development Indicators 2011,* Table 2.15, *Education Gaps by Income and Gender*.

[17]See above ADB (2012, document 16, p. 65).

[18]See OECD (2011, pp. 57–59).

[19]See above ADB (2012, documents 16, p. 65).

[20]There are diverse forms of this "rent-seeking" behavior: hidden or open government transfer, subsidies or laws to reduce market competition, lax enforcement of competition related laws, and laws to allow organizations to transfer costs.

[21]See above ADB (2012, document 16, p. 56).

[22]See Li (2010).

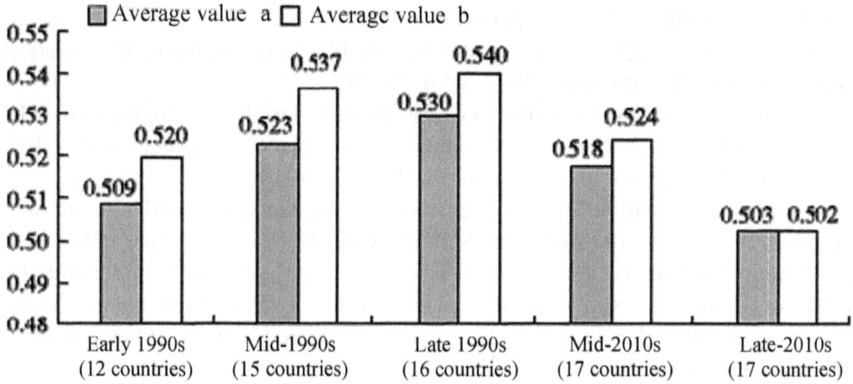

Fig. 1.1 Inequality in Latin America (Gini coefficient) in the Period from the 1990s to the First Decade of the 21st Century. *Note* The above average values refer to weighted average. Average value **a** covers all countries, and the average value **b** only includes countries with reduced inequality in the first ten years of the 21st century. *Source* Lustig et al. (2011) Fig. 1.2

health expenditure.[23] Health spending in several middle-income countries is below the average of all nations in this group. It should be 5.7% of GDP, but is 4.1% in India and 2.6% in Indonesia. This is also shown in per capita expenditure (purchasing power parity): the average data of middle-income countries in this regard is USD369, while that of India and Indonesia is USD132 and USD112 respectively.[24]

1.3 Addressing Inequality in Middle-Income Countries: Policy, Practice and Case Studies

In order to identify relevant policies to reverse worsening inequality, it is necessary to briefly talk about the middle-income countries that have been successful in improving their situation and identify the reasons for their success.

In the 1980s and early 1990s, income inequality increased in many Latin American countries. However, since the mid-1990s, especially in the first decade of the current century, income inequality has declined, while increasing in other middle-income countries. It should be noted that, despite a decline, the level of inequality remains high. However, this relatively large-scale reversal still deserves our careful study.

Changes in inequality are measured by per capita income, and specified in the Gini coefficient. The specific situation is shown in Fig. 1.1.

The decline in inequality was most pronounced in Argentina and Brazil, as well as in Chile, as shown in Table 1.4.

What caused a decline of inequality in these countries?

[23] See above Li (2012, document 24).

[24] (2010) Data come from World Bank (2012, Table 216, pp. 100–102).

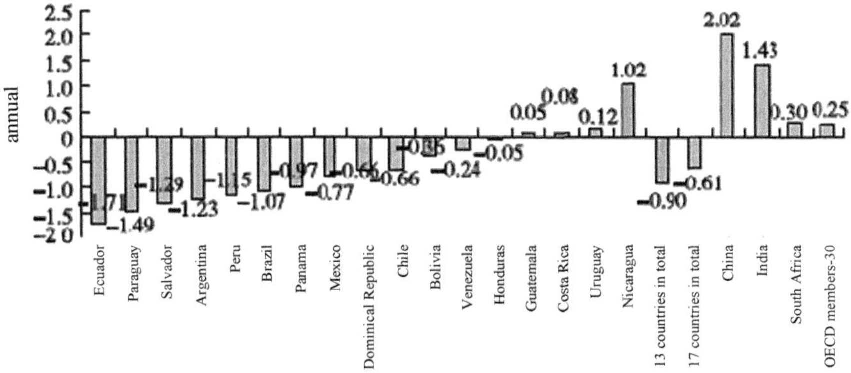

Fig. 1.2 Reduction of Inequality in Latin American Countries: 2000–2009 (Percentage change per year expressed as Gini coefficient). *Note* The table comes from Lustig (2011b)

Table 1.4 Gini coefficients for selected Latin American Countries[a]

Gene coefficient	1990	2002	2006	2010
Argentina	0.501	0.590	0.510	0.445
Brazil	0.627	0.621	0.602	0.547(2009)
Chile	0.554	0.550	0.522	0.521(2009)

[a]Data taken from World Bank, *World Development Indicators,* the annual data corresponds to the annual indicators report

For Latin America as a whole, the external trade environment has undoubtedly become more favorable. Since the beginning of the present century, the development of China and other Asian countries has exerted a great impact on global import and export trade. From 1995 to 2007, the proportion of regional exports to GDP increased from 13 to 26%, mainly benefiting from a sharp rise in prices. In addition, external financing has become easier. From 2004 to 2007, Latin America's capital inflows increased significantly. Most obvious is the investment flowing into the private sector, and the rapid development of stock and securities investment in regional stock markets.[25] These two factors have contributed to a strong economic recovery. The growth rate of many Latin American countries in the first decade of the 21st Century has increased (Brazil's current GDP growth rate is 7.2%, and Argentina's 9.2%).[26] This has paved way for reductions in poverty and inequality levels; however, we are more concerned about what has happened in these successful countries during this period. This can be understood through a brief look at the experiences of Argentina and Brazil.

[25]For example, the capitalized value of stock market in the seven regional economies quadrupled from 2004 to 2007. For more information on this trend, see Cornia (2009), as well as Ocampo (2007, pp. 7–33).

[26]Please refer to World Bank (2012).

As for Argentina, many analysts believe the main reason for the decrease in the inequality in per capita income of households is the narrowing gap in labor (earning) income, 70% of the decrease attributable to this reason. This seems to be because more unemployed people have gained access to education with the accelerated development of Argentina; at the same time, the proportion of skilled workers in the whole labor force has increased through more attention being paid to worker technical training (thus reducing the "skill premium" prevailing in the 1990s, when only a few skilled workers were involved); another factor is the expanding influence of domestic trade unions. Equally important is the country's heavy investment in the national poverty reduction program, especially the large-scale cash-oriented transfer program, the most famous of which is the *jefes y jefas de Hogar desocupados* (offering help to unemployed women and men in charge) program launched after 2002.[27] This program mainly transfers cash to families with a female head. The women need to work in small businesses after receiving further education and vocational training, or work for community projects. The program covers two million people, the spending now accounting for 5% of the national budget. According to UNDP estimation, the program has greatly promoted the rapid development of poverty reduction, with the poverty rate dropping from 9.9% in 2002 to 4.5% in 2005.

Brazil and Argentina share some of the same enablers, such as a reduction in wage inequality; however, in the case of Brazil, a reduction in wage inequality is more related to a reduction in the level of education inequality, especially at the primary and secondary levels. For example, the overall level of inequality in education fell from 0.45 in mid-2002 to 0.441 in mid-2007. Regional inequality also seems to have declined as the wage gap between big and small cities has narrowed.[28] Public transfer is also very important, and its role is mainly manifested by improving the coverage of targeted conditional cash transfers and cash transfer plans. The main cash transfer plans include the well-known *Bolsa Familia* and *Beneficio de Prestacao Continuada* (Brazilian Pension Plan).

Brazil and Argentina have common stimuli.

In the first few years of the 21st century, the proportion of skilled workers in the whole labor force began to rise to a level higher than that of the 1990s. As a result, the skill premium began to take effect, and income inequality began to decline. But most importantly, this trend had been strengthened due to the improvement of education of unskilled workers. We can clearly see that improving access to education can help reduce the level of inequality in not only that field but also removing income inequality.

Cash transfers also play a significant role in addressing inequality. For example, between 2000 and 2007, Argentina's fiscal policy focused more on redistribution, thus

---

[27] For details of the plan and its implementation, please refer to Kostzer (2008), Argentina: A Case Study on the *Plan Jefesy Jefas de Hogar Desocupados*, as well as the Employment Road to Economic Recovery, UNDP Buenos Aires.

[28] For example, the wage disparity between large and small-sized cities fell from 26% in 2000 to 19.4% in 2007. Please see Lustig (2011b, p. 14).

reducing the Gini coefficient of market income by 4.8 percentage points. If the non-cash transfer (calculated value of public education and public health) was included in the calculation, Argentina's fiscal policy actually reduced the Gini coefficient of net market income by 12.8%.[29] In addition, cash transfers also reduced the extreme poverty rate by 63%.[30] The same conclusion can be drawn from Brazil's cash transfer plan. For example, a survey in 2006 showed a reduction in inequality from 2000–2006, and concluded that one-third of the change was attributable to the government's cash transfer (pension plan and *Bolsa Familia* plan).

Large-scale cash transfers targeting the poor have been heavily used, which also depends on the increase and change in the structure of social spending. Since the mid-1990s, the overall level of social spending in Latin America has been rising. The proportion of social spending in Brazil and Argentina, for instance, reached 15–20% of GDP, which is close to the level of OECD member countries. In this growth process, the structural change of expenditure was very important, and the growth of expenditure was mainly concentrated in social insurance, social assistance and education.[31]

Finally, we need to mention the fundamental changes in tax policy. In particular, since 2002, increased income resulting from the tax policy helped promote development of the cash transfer plan. These policy changes are characteristic of Latin America as a whole. The central government's tax and non-tax revenue increased from 15 to 17% in the 1990–2000 period, and reached 20.2% in 2007. In Brazil and Argentina, the increase reached 9% between 2002 and 2007. Many think this rise is largely due to what is known as a "windfall", that is, tax growth is the result of the rise of global commodity prices; however, there should be other reasons, such as the expansion of the tax base, increase of direct tax (such as personal and corporate tax) and indirect tax (generally, value-added tax), as well as efforts to reduce evasion. As of 2006, Brazil and Argentina's tax levels were close to those of OECD countries such as Japan and the United States. This increase in income occurred alongside a reduction of external debt, with Argentina and Brazil both paying back large debts to the International Monetary Fund.

Having examined cases of these two Latin American countries in the first 10 years of the 21st century, we now have evidence to draw the following conclusions: under certain conditions, reasonable GDP growth, reduction of inequality and reduction of poverty are achievable. This can satisfy the needs of a growth mode featuring relatively strong inclusiveness (as defined by Terry McKinley).[32] If the goal of reducing educational inequality is added, there will be a growth mode with stronger inclusiveness (as defined by Campbell and others.[33]).

---

[29] See Lustig (2011a, p. 23).

[30] See Cornia (2009).

[31] It can be seen from the diagram that only Ecuador's social expenditure as a proportion of GDP in 2004–2005 was lower than that in 1990–1991.

[32] See McKinley (2010).

[33] Please see Kanbur and Raunyar (2009).

Based on the evaluation of middle-income countries in Latin America and the conclusion that growth, inequality and poverty are closely interrelated in other middle-income countries, what policy changes are possible in order to solve the current inequality in middle-income countries and achieve a more inclusive growth and development mode?

1.4 The Need for a Diversity of Policies to Reduce Inequality

1.4.1 Addressing Regional Inequalities

Case studies made previously on middle-income countries show that regional disparities play a role in contributing to persistent inequality. However, the Asian Development Bank recently conducted a new study from a more macro angle, and revealed that, in Asia, 30–50% of income inequality was caused by unbalanced growth.[34] This clearly shows that addressing regional inequality is closely related to the change from being a middle-income country to a high-income one.[35] With the socio-economic development of a country, the regional gap will gradually disappear, especially when compared with welfare. A World Bank study (2009) divides each studied country into five regions and measures the welfare gap in each region. The per capita GDP of Bangladesh and Cambodia is less than USD300 (2000 data). The welfare gap between the richest and poorest regions of the two countries is 89% and 73% respectively; for Colombia and Thailand (each with a per capita GDP of USD2000), the gap is close to 50%; for Canada (per capita GDP USD20,000), the gap is less than 25%.[36]

Solving regional inequalities like this, however, means recognizing that inequality in each of the middle-income countries, and the reasons behind this problem, vary greatly. For example, the gap between different regions in India reflects the unbalanced development of various states; the inequality in China finds expression mainly in the gap between various provinces; and regional gap in South Africa that previously affected by racial segregation is closely related to moral and racial inequality. As we all know, if we develop export-oriented production areas in regions with advantages in natural resources, regional inequality will increase, which is clearly shown in Latin America in the 1970s and 1980s and China in the 1990s. Some of the main characteristics of disadvantaged areas include low levels of human capital, infrastructure, and the accessibility of social and public services. In order to solve these problems, two aspects of work have special importance: fiscal transfers from a rich region to a poor one, and the formulation of a practical regional growth strategy. What middle-income

[34] See Asian Development Bank (2012, p. 74).

[35] For data, see World Bank (2009).

[36] See World Bank (2009, pp. 88–89).

countries need to pay attention to is, of course, the core of the Western region development strategy of the Chinese Government. Many studies have shown that the Chinese Government's strategy launched in 2000 has accelerated the growth of the eleven provinces covered, and has, since 2004, led to reduced inequality.[37] The strategy for the development of western region focuses on infrastructure development (such as power, transportation and communications) in major regions, but its focus is a large financial transfer from the central government, creating favorable conditions for the subsequent foreign direct investment. In the 1970s, Malaysia began to work to solve the rising poverty rate of each state through financial transfers, mainly in the fields of health and education. By the early 1980s, the gap between states with the highest and lowest poverty rates had dropped from 60 to 18%.[38] Other important cases show some middle-income countries have focused on regional inequality through specific welfare plans based on changing forms of fiscal transfer. For example, in the field of health, the coefficient of variation of the average learning level in Indonesian provinces decreased from 0.43 in 1971 to 0.15 in 2000.[39] Similarly, in Thailand, thanks to targeted fiscal transfers, gap in terms of the infant mortality rate between Thailand's least developed and developed regions was 6% in 1980 and 0.7% in 2000.[40]

1.4.2 Addressing Inequalities in Health and Education

As mentioned earlier, government spending on health and education can help reduce inequality in both areas. Apart from what has been outlined before, a recent comparison group estimated the situation of 150 countries in the period 1970–2001 and came to the conclusion that increasing investment in education and health can significantly reduce the Gini coefficient,[41] a conclusion which is identical with case studies in Brazil and Argentina referred to earlier. In India, China and Indonesia, government investment accounts for only 4% of total spending in education and 5% in health (compared to an average of 5.2 and 9.4% in OECD countries respectively). Therefore, middle-income countries should increase their investment in the two fields. Given their fast development, they should be able to achieve their goal in this regard.

[37] Most famous relevant documents: Fan et al. (2011, pp. 47–56). Also see Fan et al. (eds.) (2009).

[38] The data come from Malaysia's Ministry of Economic Planning in 2008 and quoted in World Bank (2009, p. 27).

[39] See Hill et al. (2007).

[40] See Wisaweisuan (2009).

[41] Please refer to Claus, Iris, Martinez-Vazquez, Jorge, Vulovic, Violetta, Government Fiscal Policies and Redistribution in Asian Countries, International Center for Public Policy Working Paper 12–13, *Andrew Young School of Policy Studies,* Georgia State University. According to the document, Asia's investment in education has helped reduced the inequality in the field and is much better than in other parts of the world in this regard; however, Asia's investment in health is not as good as in other countries in the world (see document p. 25).

However, the main problem here is the target population - even if health and education facilities are good and complete, poor families may not be able to afford them. So, programs such as conditional cash transfers are very important, as illustrated by the cases of Brazil and Argentina, which have been very successful in improving the enrolment of poor family members.

Conditional cash transfer (CCT) has also been implemented in South Africa, Nigeria, Indonesia and other middle-income countries; however, China and India still haven't implemented it on a large scale.[42] Yet, while the CCT remains quite popular as an effective short-term measure, what its long-term impacts are not yet clear. For example, even though CCT allows more children from poor families easier access to hospital, it does not necessarily improve their nutritional level.[43] In addition, recent data show that, in some cases, such as in Bangladesh, the eligibility criteria leave many who are poor unable to benefit.[44] Some gains might have been made, but any improvement may have been derived from the Multidimensional Poverty Index to specify broader eligibility criteria, which has been used by Ghana, which recently implemented CCT to stimulate the enrollment rate of primary education.

1.4.3 Changes in Fiscal Policy

Efforts to mitigate regional inequality and overall human capital inequality may impose a heavy fiscal burden on the government. Thus, there is the need to increase income to finance the two objectives simultaneously, while at the same time ensuring that the social security system is adequately funded. Below we look at the experiences of selected countries. As in what Brazil and Argentina have done demonstrates, in order to increase income, some middle-income countries have needed to make significant changes to their fiscal policies. The main problem here is how to improve redistribution while ensuring growth, and effectively reduce inequality. Brazil's experience underscores the importance of simplifying the tax system, and expanding the tax base, especially by including more of the informal sectors. What the Latin American countries have done offers other middle-income countries an example of how to achieve a balance among individual income tax, property tax and consumption tax. When the consumption tax and income tax do manage to achieve such a balance, the tax revenues produced become more progressive, thereby reducing income inequality. This is particularly true in India, a middle-income country where the proportion of the population who pay personal income taxes remains low—between 2 and 3% in recent years. Obviously, changes in taxation—such as including the informal sector to tackle tax evasion and introducing a more progressive tax system—can help increase

[42]China's "basic living allowance" program is a basic cash transfer, with no restrictions, and the only condition is that recipients are very poor.

[43]Please refer to Fiszbein and Schady (2009).

[44]For more related data, please refer to Slater and Farrington (2009).

revenues and reduce income inequality. However, it still takes time to produce favorable changes in taxation system through implementation of these policies. Very often, there will be political hurdles. This is especially true with some middle-income countries that rely heavily on resource development, as they can increase their income at a faster rate in the short term if they rely on increasing taxes on raw material exports. In view of the time limit, in addition to CCT, only clearly targeted social welfare and social protection programs can help solve inequality problems more comprehensively in the short term.

1.4.4 Improving Social Protection

Available data show that social protection programs are crucial in reducing inequality. These programs play a significant role in meeting the needs of the poor families and solving transitional poverty; however, the coverage and expenditure of social protection in many middle-income countries remain far behind those in high-income countries.

Middle income countries, such as Brazil and Russia, spend 15–20% of their GDP on social protection programs, while countries such as India and China spend much less—an average of 5–7% in recent years. In contrast, OECD member countries spent 20% of their GDP on social protection programs in 2007.[45]

Different middle-income countries have achieved different social protection coverage. For example, Brazil has a comprehensive social insurance program, funded by individual contributions. This program covers pensions, maternity, disability and work-related injury insurance. In Brazil, there is also unemployment insurance. In contrast, the coverage of social protection in India is very limited. Only a certain degree of medical insurance and maternity allowance cover employees with higher wages, with a total coverage of only nine million. In addition to the small individual contribution social security scheme operated by the government, India has very limited employment plans and basic food subsidies.

Unemployment programs in middle-income countries generally focus on basic severance payments, while support for existing unemployment insurance is low. One reason for the limited support for unemployment insurance is that employment rates are concentrated in companies that do not pay the minimum unemployment insurance premiums, and companies refusing to pay severance payments.[46] Some middle-income countries also have exceptionally high eligibility standards. In India, for example, workers have to pay for at least five years before they can begin to enjoy any benefits. Among the total number of employees, the proportion of people

---

[45]Data come from OECD (2011), *Divided We Stand: Why Inequality Keeps Rising*, OECD, Paris.

[46]For example, in Indonesia (2008), 34 percent of workers entitled to severance payments have received the pay after they were laid out. Most of them received less than they deserved. See World Bank (2010).

receiving insurance is as low as only 10%. South Africa and China are good examples of this.[47]

In addition to the conditional cash transfers mentioned above, middle-income countries have other non-individual payment schemes, such as food, municipal engineering, labor and job creation. India has the largest municipal engineering program in the world, covering about 10% of the workforce. Another case in point is Indonesia, where jobs were created for about 5% of the workforce between 2000 and 2006.[48]

When we examine how to improve social protection programs, we have already outlined the role of CCT, including its role in creating more education equality. However, there is another major problem in the area of social protection, namely, policies on employment and unemployment.

Middle-income countries will have to spend longer time to expand the coverage of their unemployment compensation programs if they are to match the current level of high-income countries. This is because the effort requires a lot of capital expenditure, and as the government employs a large number of people working in the informal (and immigrant) sector, problems will arise. As mentioned earlier, Brazil has a relatively generous unemployment compensation scheme with a wide coverage. Other middle-income countries should also refer to Brazil's experience, especially the target of its scheme. Compensation is paid out to workers who have been unfairly laid off, or who have lost their jobs as a result of a factory closure. It also focuses on workers in families mostly in need based on the evaluation of funds available to workers at the time of dismissal. In addition, sustained support is conditional for the unemployed who must prove they are doing their best to find a new job. For middle-income countries with limited social spending, but who want to expand their unemployment compensation schemes, what Brazil has done or is still doing could be a valuable reference. Once established, the eligibility criteria can be gradually relaxed, but in the initial year(s), Brazil's approach may be more appropriate.

For social protection and employment, the minimum wage policy is very important, mainly because redistribution of income to workers at the bottom of the wage system can narrow the income gap and even stimulate demand. In the case of Brazil and Argentina, the informal sector also works when the minimum wage is ensured in the formal sector. At present, the minimum wage policy of the middle-income countries has a relatively narrow coverage. Compared with other middle-income countries and high-income countries, the minimum wage in India and China is very low. For example, the minimum wage bottom line in India is about 21% of the average domestic wage; in China, it is 24%. The data basically refer to the urban sector, so have little impact on the informal work system and have no relevance to rural areas. Given the high level of inequality in the two countries, where redistribution can have a certain impact, it is necessary to raise the minimum wage.

We have so far proposed several ways to improve social protection work, mainly focusing on a few specific plans. At present, a key issue for middle-income countries is that many of the plans so far implemented are too decentralized to achieve the

[47] See OECD (2011, p. 60).

[48] Please refer to World Bank (2010).

desired level of cooperation or coordination. Generally speaking, there is little cooperation between social insurance and social assistance, and little coordination within the plan. Let us take the pension sector as an example. There are usually different but overlapping uncoordinated plans targeting different groups, such as those for workers in the rural, public and private sectors. Therefore, the government should work to reduce such dispersion and improve the degree of integration and harmony.[49] This is expected to improve the efficiency and overall function of social protection. For example, it is good to unite health insurance with pension plans so as to motivate people to save for the future; integrate long-term savings and unemployment benefits so as to better protect workers against a possible recession; and combine some plans to save scarce resources and ensure financing and management become more efficient.

Cooperation and coordination among social protection plans in middle-income countries can be demonstrated by the level of development and the coverage of individual plans, as well as through the degree of coordination and integration among plans. In the beginning, some plans espousing the same goal can be integrated. On this basis, many plans can also be coordinated in a broader scope because of the same authorization and tools being used, financing mechanisms and institutional arrangements. In general, the goal is to promote plan coordination by increasing inclusiveness, and, on this basis, hopefully improve the fairness of the insurance arrangements. Improving coordination is good for most middle-income countries, even if the levels of their social protection are very different. This can be shown by the examples of India and China.

India's social protection coverage is very low, mainly focusing on solving the problem of long-term poverty. It mainly covers the rural population through the food plan and basic support. For example, the Indian government spends 2% of its GDP on social protection programs every year, and 50% of this goes on food and fuel subsidies. Other social protection programs implemented by the government are very limited, generally providing support for rural housing, school meals and medical insurance subsidies. Generally speaking, these plans have no relationship to each other, and there is little cooperation or coordination between them. In this case, increasing integration can lead to more efficient systems, which can expand coverage. For example, the design and introduction of an overall cash transfer plan can bring benefits, providing a foundation for other schemes to be carried out, such as pension plans for low-income workers through health insurance based on government subsidized long-term savings. Microfinance for beneficiaries of cash transfer and savings schemes can also be linked to the above arrangements. In recent years, the Indian government seems to be moving along this path, focusing more on cash support than food-based programs. It may combine the cash transfer plan with the existing pension plan, strengthening connection in these areas, and ensuring provision of a sound municipal engineering plan for the beneficiaries of cash transfers.

[49]These problems are detailed in the literature: Robalino et al. (2012). The following discussion also draws on some of its conclusions.

Compared with India, China's social protection plan has a wider coverage and scope. This is also true in terms with China's pension, medical insurance, unemployment insurance, minimum living insurance and education subsidy. However, the coverage and quantity of these plans vary greatly between urban and rural areas and among various provinces. There are also some differences among the people who most need these plans. For example, in 2010, the subsistence allowances in urban areas were more than double those offered in rural areas; the level of pension provision in rural areas was also relatively low, and there were variations between cities. The household registration system currently prevailing in China restricts the social resources and welfare available to migrant workers, thus social protection needs to become fairer and more transferable, and, by improving coordination and integration between different plans, work to promote faster materialization in achieving this goal. At present, China has different medical security systems to cover urban workers, urban unemployed and urban and rural residents with economic difficulties. These systems are designed separately, and their respective regulatory systems are also independent of each other. They cover only 29% of the fifteen million migrant workers in China. In such circumstances, it is obvious China needs a higher degree of harmony and a wider coverage for more effective management and solution of the inequality caused by the household registration system. Similarly, in terms of the pension system, urban residents enjoy a variety of programs, while the government in rural areas pays basic pension (different standards prevailing in different regions). At present, only a quarter of migrant workers enjoy endowment insurance (the coverage rate of urban permanent workers is 80%), and only 35% of rural workers are insured.[50] China offers a variety of pension schemes for all kinds of people—staff of state-owned enterprises and public institutions, civil servants, urban and rural residents and migrant workers. These all operate separately without taking into consideration that the target recipients may move from one sector to another. People involved in these schemes differ greatly in wages and their remuneration has poor transparency. The schemes for urban and rural employees, employees of state-owned enterprises and institutions, and urban residents cannot be transferred to each other.[51] If they can be integrated, it may be of greater benefit for them. For example, if efforts could be first made to integrate the policy framework and management of the three schemes for employees, civil servants and urban employees of state-owned enterprises and institutions, and then work to integrate the schemes for urban and rural residents in Beijing, Shanghai and Zhongshan of Guangdong, where the schemes have already been largely integrated. The integration of the schemes can help build up a firm foundation for a higher level of financing, and also help with better exchange of information on financing, beneficiaries and other aspects. This will help achieve the main goal—making the transfer between schemes more efficient and strengthen insurance fairness. In addition, improving the coordination and integration among social security, medical insurance and endowment insurance can help improve social security, enhance household consumer confidence, reduce the high savings rate to

[50]Data come from World Bank (2012, p. 372).

[51]There is a certain degree of transferability in urban employee insurance scheme.

meet emergencies, and thus stimulate people's consumption—therefore improving the level of demand and helping China rebalance its economy.

1.5 Summary

To sum up, the following major policy areas can be considered by middle-income countries in addressing persistent inequality.

(1) Formulate and implement comprehensive regional development strategies, which should stress infrastructure development and coordinated government involvement to strengthen the coverage of the electric power, transportation and communication sectors. These strategies should be supported by fiscal transfers to encourage domestic and foreign direct investment. This fiscal transfer should focus on the areas of health and education.
(2) Significantly increase human capital expenditure in health and education. This task has become much easier in recent years because of the satisfactory development of middle-income countries overall. Policies to increase spending in these areas should be particularly targeted at poor communities and families, where cash transfers can be a successful bridge. However, more policies are needed to ensure the sustainability of cash transfers, and data show this is an important issue plaguing middle-income countries.
(3) Change and formulate fiscal policies to simplify the tax system and expand the coverage, so as to make it possible for tax collection to cover the relatively large informal sectors. At the same time, efforts should be made to shift the balance from consumption to income, thus introducing more progressive methods.
(4) Promote important changes in social protection plans. First of all, there is a need to substantially raise the level of existing social spending, and then, under this overall framework, expand the coverage of social protection plans. In the area of unemployment benefits, in particular, there is a need for change—to expand coverage and to target benefits more efficiently to those most in need. Similarly, the minimum wage standard can be raised, while dispersion among plans is also an important problem to be solved. However, the key lies in the fact that there are many reasons for the current decentralization of plans of various middle-income countries. Moreover, as reasons vary with various countries, remedies should be adopted on the basis of the existing coverage and local conditions. So far as India is concerned, it can strengthen its integration by designing and introducing an overall cash transfer plan. On the basis of this overall cash transfer plan, more arrangements can be developed, such as the pension schemes for low-income workers worked out on the foundation provided by medical insurance based on government subsidy and long-term savings. In contrast, China has a relatively wider coverage. The main problem is that, as the movement between different sectors is limited, and there is a large gap between them, transfers under social protection plans is difficult, and the transparency is very low. These problems

can be solved by enhancing integration. At first, it is important to integrate the management of social security, medical security and pension plans, and, on the basis, expand the integration of urban and rural residents' plans initially implemented.

References

Asian Development Bank (ADB). (2012). *Asian development outlook 2012: Confronting rising inequality in Asia* (p. 2012). Manila: ADB.

Berg, O., & Zettelmeyer (2008). *What makes growth sustained?* (IMF Working Paper 08/59). Washington, DC: IMF.

Berg, A. G., & Ostry, J. D. (2011). *Inequality and unsustainable growth: Two sides of the same coin?*. IMF: Washington, DC.

Chandy, L., & Geertz, C. (2011). *Poverty in numbers: The changing state of global poverty from 2005 to 2015.* The Brookings Institution: Washington, DC.

Claus, I., Martinez-Vazquez, J., & Vulovic, V. *Government Fiscal Policies and Redistribution in Asian Countries, International Center for Public Policy Working Paper 12–13.* Andrew Young School of Policy Studies, Georgia State University.

Cornia, G. A. (2009). What explains the recent decline of income inequality in Latin America, draft paper presented to The Conference on the Impact of the Financial Crisis in India, Tata Institute of Social Sciences, Mumbai, March 2009.

Fan, S., Kanbur, R., & Zhang, X. (Eds.). (2009). *Regional inequality in China: trends, explanations and policy responses.* London and New York: Routledge.

Fan, S., Kanbur, R., Zhang, X. (2011). China's regional disparities: Experience and policy. *Review of Development Finance, 1*(1).

Fiszbein, A., & Schady, N. (2009). *Conditional cash transfers: Reducing present and future poverty* (World Bank Policy Research Report). Washington, DC.

Gill, I., & Kharas, H., (2007). *An East Asian renaissance: Ideas for economic growth.* Washington, DC: World Bank.

Hill, H., Resosudarmo, B., & Vidyattama, Y. (2007). *Indonesia's changing economic geography* (Working Papers in Economics and Development Studies, 2007–2013). Bandung, Indonesia.

Kanbur, R., & Raunyar, G. (2009). Conceptualizing inclusive development: With applications to rural infrastructure and development assistance. Asian Development Bank, Occasional Paper No.7, 2007, ADB, Manila.

Kostzer, D. (2008). *Argentina: A Case Study on the Plan Jefes y Jefas de Hogar Desocupados, or the Employment Road to Economic Recovery.* UNDP Buenos Aires.

Li, X. (2010). *China: Rural statistics 2010.* Beijing: China Agricultural Press.

Li, S., & Luo, C. (2011). *Introduction to Overview: Income Inequality and Poverty in China, 2002–2007, CBI Working Paper 2011–2010,* Department of Economics, University of Western Ontario, Canada.

Lustig, N. (2011a). Fiscal policy and income redistribution in Latin America: Challenging the conventional wisdom. Society for the Study of Economic Inequality.

Lustig, N. (2011b). Markets, the state and inclusive growth in Latin America: Argentina, Brazil, Mexico and Peru. UNDP.

Lustig, N. et al. (2011). *The decline in inequality in Latin America: How much, since, when and why* (Working Paper, No. 118). Tulane University, Canada.

McKinley, T. (2010). *Inclusive Growth Criteria and Indicators: An Inclusive Growth Index for Diagnosis of Country Progress* (Asian Development Bank, Sustainable Development Working Paper 14). Manila.

Ocampo, J. A. (2007). The Latin American boom. *Revista de Ciencia Politica, 28*(1).
Organisation for Economic Co-operation and Development(OECD). (2011). *Divided we stand: Why inequality keeps rising*. Paris: OECD.
Ravallion, M., & Chen. (2004). *China's (Uneven) progress against poverty* (World Bank Policy Research Working Paper 3408). Washington, DC: World Bank.
Robalino, D. A., Rawlings, L., & Walker, I. (2012). *Building social protection and labor systems: Concepts and operational implications* (Social Protection and Labor Discussion Paper No. 1202). Washington, DC: World Bank.
Slater, Rachel, & Farrington, John. (2009). *Cash transfers: Targeting*. London: ODI Project Briefing, Overseas Development Institute.
Stiglitz, Joseph E. (2010). *Freefall: America, Free markets and the sinking of the world economy*. New York: Norton.
Stiglitz, J. E. (2012). *The price of inequality*. London: Allen Lane.
Sumner, A. (2012, May). *Global poverty and the 'New bottom billion revisited: Exploring the paradox that most of the world's extreme poor no longer live in the world's poorest countries* (Working Paper).
United Nations Development Programme (UNDP). (2010). *Human development report 2010: The real wealth of nations: Pathways to human development*. New York: UNDP.
United Nations Development Programme (UNDP). (2011). *Human development report 2011: Sustainability and equity: A better future for all*. New York: UNDP.
Wisaweisuan, N. (2009) Spatial disparities in Thailand: Does government policy aggravate or alleviate the problem. In *Reshaping economic geography in East Asia, Yukon Huang and Alessandro Magnoli Bocchi*. Washington, DC: World Bank.
World Bank. (2006). *World development report 2006: Equality and development*. Washington, DC: World Bank.
World Bank. (2009). *World development report 2009: Reshaping economic geography*. Washington, DC: World Bank.
World Bank. (2010). *Indonesia jobs report: Towards better jobs and security for all*, Washington, DC: World Bank.
World Bank. (2012). *World development indicators*. Washington, DC: World Bank.

Chapter 2
Inclusive Growth and Poverty Reduction of China: Progress and Main Policies

Chengwei Huang

2.1 Inclusive Growth in China: Experience and Key Features

The concept of inclusive growth has always been followed in the course of China's reform and opening up and modernization drive, showing different characteristics at different stages of development. China's inclusive growth course in the period of the reform and opening up can be divided into the following three stages.

2.1.1 Reform of the Economic System Promotes Rapid Economic Growth and Drives Large-Scale Poverty Reduction Across the Country (1978–2001)

At the beginning of China's reform and opening up introduced in late 1978, one-third of the Chinese population had insufficient food and clothing, generally living in a state of poverty and backwardness. The primary goal of economic and social development at that time was to address the problem of widespread poverty. In 1978, the Chinese government shifted its focus of work onto socialist modernization and economic development, and gradually promoted reform of economic system. During this period, the salient feature of inclusive development focused on economic development, promoting economic growth through institutional reform, and achieving nationwide large-scale poverty alleviation.

China's reform of the rural economic system was based on the household contract responsibility system implemented in the early 1980s. By 1983, land system reform

C. Huang (✉)
International Poverty Reduction Center in China, Beijing, China
e-mail: hcw65@126.com

C. Zuo et al. (eds.), *Inclusive Development and Poverty Reduction*,
International Research on Poverty Reduction,
https://doi.org/10.1007/978-981-15-8446-6_2

covered more than 98% of rural households. At the same time, the government increased the purchase price of agricultural products and gradually liberalized the pricing system. As to the reform of the distribution of agricultural products, the government first reduced the barriers and broke down the dual urban-rural structure, allowing the trade of agricultural and sideline products to replace the central government-controlled cotton and oil purchases in urban and rural areas, and encouraging the establishment of an agricultural products market in large cities. With the success of the household contract responsibility system, the government began to guide farmers to engage in diversified agricultural production and began to encourage farmers to develop cash crop production on the basis of not slackening grain production, while taking into account local natural conditions. In order to increase output, it launched large-scale agricultural science and technology research and established a national promotion system, laying a solid foundation for increased agricultural production.

Reform of the urban economic system was fully launched in October 1984, with the focus on state-owned enterprises. All were required to pay taxes instead of submitting their profits to the administration, and a breakthrough was made in the field of autonomous rights in business operations by gradually establishing the factory manager responsibility, enterprise contract management responsibility and shareholding systems. After 1992, the deep-seated contradictions accumulated by the state-owned enterprises over a prolonged-period of time were gradually exposed, forcing them to reform and seek ways to cope with market competition. The status of the non-public sectors of the economy were strengthened correspondingly along with the deepening of the reform of state-owned enterprises. In 1987, the government proposed an economic model featuring "government regulates the market while the market guides the enterprises" and the concept of a "socialist commodity economy". After 1992, the socialist market economy system was formally established and developed. From then on, the single structure of a planned economy began to change, and the new principal part of the market started to emerge.

Since the reform and opening up, China has seen rapid economic growth due to the gradual shift of its work focus to economic development, with the average annual growth rate of GDP exceeding 9%. Thanks to the "trickle-down effect", economic growth has brought about an improvement in the living standards of the poor. According to the government's poverty standards, the population living in absolute poverty fell from 250 million in 1978 to 29.27 million in 2001, and the corresponding incidence of poverty reduced from 30.7 to 3.2%. The late 1990s saw accelerated economic growth. During this period, the Chinese government began to implement planned development-oriented poverty alleviation programs, and formulated a Seven-Year Program for Lifting 80 Million People Out of Poverty (1994–2000). As a result, the poverty-stricken population declined sharply, with the incidence of poverty falling from 8.8% in 1993 to 3.4% in 2000.[1]

[1]Zhang (2007a).

2.1.2 Policy Adjustment Promotes Overall Planning of Urban and Rural Areas and Drives Balanced Development (2002–2010)

From the 1990s, the economy entered a period of sustained rapid growth. However, in the process of industrialization, the issues of agriculture, rural areas and farmers became increasingly prominent, and rural development obviously lagged behind industrial development. The result was a weak agricultural infrastructure, backward development of rural social undertakings, and a widening income gap between urban and rural residents. The salient feature of inclusive growth at this stage was that policy adjustment was made to solve the issues of "agriculture, rural areas and farmers", and to achieve overall planning of urban and rural areas and promote balanced development.

In 2002, the government adjusted the economic development strategy in the 11th Five-Year Plan for National Economic and Social Development (2006–2010), and declared that China had entered a development stage characterized by industry promoting agriculture and urban areas helping rural areas as a whole, creating favorable conditions for strengthening the support to agriculture, rural areas and farmers.

At the beginning of the 21st century, the government introduced a series of policies to benefit farmers, including adjusting the structure of national income distribution, fiscal expenditure, investment in fixed assets, and credit supply. It expanded the scope of rural areas covered by public finance, and increased the supply of rural public goods. It also established a unified labor market in urban and rural areas, removed restrictions on farmers' employment in cities, carried out training for the labor force involved in transfer employment, and solved prominent problems such as wage arrears for migrant workers and social security for them, and further clarified the responsibility of governments at all levels for rural compulsory education. Work was undertaken to increase State financial investment in the rural cooperative medical care system, and establish a serious illness insurance coordination mechanism. Efforts were made to establish a fair and unified social welfare system in urban and rural areas, implement the rural minimum living allowance system, and improve the rural social relief system.[2]

In 2001, the central government began pilot rural tax reform, and fully implemented the reform in 2003, aiming to alleviate the burden on farmers and prevent the aggravation of unreasonable charges in rural areas. In 2004, it was proposed to gradually reduce the agricultural tax rate until the agricultural tax was completely abolished. In 2006, the agricultural tax was completely abolished nationwide.

These policies for benefiting farmers laid a foundation for stable and sustainable agricultural development, basically solving food and clothing shortages for farmers and meeting their basic daily needs. Living standards were greatly improved, and the

[2]Zhang Lei (2011). *The Evolution of China's Development-Oriented Poverty Alleviation Policy (1949-2005)*, China Financial and Economic Publishing House).

process of poverty reduction in rural areas accelerated. During this period, China's rural poor population showed a decentralized trend, and the government adjusted the rural poverty alleviation methods and strategies accordingly, and formulated *The Outline for Development-Oriented Poverty Alleviation for China's Rural Areas (2001–2010)*, according to which it shifted its poverty reduction targets from poverty-stricken counties to poverty-stricken villages, directly benefiting the poorest people. This led to a fall in the poverty-stricken population from 58.25 million in 2002 (low-income population only) to 26.88 million in 2010.[3]

2.1.3 Building an Institutional System Promotes Inclusive Growth and Boosts Comprehensive, Coordinated and Sustainable Economic and Social Development (Since 2011)

Since the reform and opening up, the strategies of unbalanced growth—"focusing on the central task of economic construction" and "encouraging some people and some areas to become rich first, and helping the poor areas and people get rich to achieve common prosperity" have played a crucial role in launching economic system reform and boosting the economic takeoff. However, the unbalanced development mechanism did cause a widening gap between rich and poor, with regional disparities, and urban-rural disparities. The proportion of investment going to basic people's livelihood in GDP is still relatively low, leading to economic growth that depends on investment and exports, and insufficient consumer motivation. This also caused a series of problems such as difficulties and high expense in medical care, imbalanced education, and insufficient supply of public infrastructure facilities. These social problems even affected social equity, justice and stability.

Against this background, the government clearly put forward and actively advocated the concept of inclusive growth. With the goal of building a moderately prosperous society in all aspects, it sought comprehensive, coordinated and sustainable economic and social development to realize development is for the people, and that its fruits are shared by the people. To this end, it proposed the strategic task of "building a harmonious socialist society", and worked hard to maintain balance between urban and rural development, development of different regions, economic and social development, man and nature, and domestic development and opening to the outside world. Meanwhile, efforts were made to accelerate the sound development of the national economy, and strengthen social construction focusing on improving people's livelihood, and attaching more importance to the people-oriented principle, comprehensive, coordinated and sustainable development, overall planning, and the work of ensuring and improving people's livelihood and promoting social equity and justice.

---

[3]National Bureau of Statistics. *Rural Poverty Monitoring*, 2010.

Inclusive growth at this stage was achieved mainly by improving various systems, and integrating successful pilot policies into national development plans to form a sound institutional system. Specific efforts included transforming the development mode from one featuring high investment, high consumption, high emissions, difficult recycling and low efficiency, to an emphasis on energy saving, emission reduction, environmental protection and land conservation; comprehensively promoting economic, political, cultural, and social development and reform to ensure they were coordinated and mutually adaptable, especially highlighting social construction with a focus on improving people's livelihood, and solving the problems of groups facing difficulties in education, medical care and housing; and adjusting income distribution policies, maintaining social fairness and justice and promoting sustainable and rapid economic development.

In the coming decade, China will take the development-oriented poverty alleviation drive as a long-term historical task "concerning the overall situation of socialist modernization drive", and begin to implement the 12th Five-Year Plan and the Outline for Development-oriented Poverty Reduction for China's Rural Areas (2011–2020). The government has set a poverty reduction goal for the next decade as enabling those being targeted to be free from worries about food and clothing, and ensuring compulsory education for their children, basic medical care and housing. Since the remaining population in absolute poverty is mainly distributed in fourteen contiguous poor areas with special difficulties represented by the Wuling Mountain area, Liupan Mountain area and Qinba Mountain area, the government takes them as the main battlefields for the development-oriented poverty alleviation drive.

2.2 Main Policies Promoting Inclusive Growth in China

2.2.1 Adjusting and Optimizing the Industrial Structure, and Emphatically Promoting the Transformation of the Economic Development Model

Thanks to more than thirty years of development, China has realized the transformation from a low-income country to a middle-income one by adopting a series of policies such as industrial restructuring. In order to stabilize this achievement and achieve greater development, the government has begun to accelerate the process of transforming the economic growth model.

Main policies on industrial restructuring. Through industrial, fiscal and tax policies and industry access, China channels more funds to the weak links and high-tech industries. In 2009, it implemented a plan for the adjustment and revitalization of the top ten key industries. In that year, China arranged some RMB20 billion of special funds for technological transformation to support 4,441 projects. It is estimated that by 2020, the total added value of six emerging industries including information and communications, advanced equipment manufacturing, new materials, new energy and energy conservation and environmental protection, bio-industry and high-end productive service industry will account for about 20% of GDP.[4]

As for the main policy of transforming the economic growth model, in order to avoid the "middle-income trap", the 11th Five-Year Plan released in 2006 explicitly proposed "speeding up the transformation of economic growth model". Eight binding indicators were adopted to measure the transformation of economic growth model, including energy and environmental protection indicators and indicators covering the areas of people's livelihood such as population control, endowment insurance and rural medical care. Economic growth, which was most valued previously, was included in the category of expected indicators.

Through industrial restructuring and the initial transformation of the economic growth model, the endogenous driving force of the Chinese economy was thus enhanced, and the economic structure became more reasonable. According to the data released by the National Bureau of Statistics, during the 11th Five-Year Plan, the proportion of employed persons in the tertiary industry in social employment increased from 31.4% in 2005 to 33.2% in 2008. In 2009, the proportion of the value added of the tertiary industry in China's GDP rose from 40.3% at the end of the 10th Five-Year Plan period to 42.6%.[5]

2.2.2 Improving the Quality and Ability of Workers, and Creating More Employment and Development Opportunities

2.3 Employment and Social Security Policies for Migrant Population

The Chinese government's migrant population policy was implemented in three stages: in the 1980s, the free flow of farmers was somewhat restricted for a long time mainly through the dual urban-rural household registration system. After the 1990s, the rural surplus labor force, however, was encouraged to seek jobs in urban areas, with the government providing employment training and services. Now, in the 21st century, the reform of the household registration system and social security policies concerning elderly care, medical care, housing and children's education have been steadily implemented to promote integration of migrant population into urban development (for specific policies,please see Table 2.1).

The policy changes from control to encouragement and provision of services have accelerated the autonomous flow of large numbers of the surplus rural labor force to urban areas across the country. These people now constitute the main force engaged in secondary and tertiary industries in urban areas. According to the statistical bulletin

[4]Ma (2011).

[5]See Footnote 4.

Table 2.1 Evolution of policies for migrant population

Release time	Title	Policy highlights
March 1989	Emergency Notice of the General Office of the State Council on Strict Control of Migrant Workers' Going Out	Flow control
April 1989	Notice of the Ministry of Civil Affairs and the Ministry of Public Security on Further Control of the Blind Outflow of Migrant Workers	Flow control
April 1990	Notice of the State Council on Doing a Good Job in Employment	Employment encouragement
November 1994	Interim Provisions of the Ministry of Labor on Inter-provincial Mobile Employment of Rural Laborers	Flow permission
1995	Opinions Forwarded by the General Offices of the CPC Central Committee and the State Council on Strengthening the Management over Migrant Population—Promoting the Local Transfer of Rural Surplus Labor Force	Flow encouragement
1999	Interim Regulations on Collection and Payment of Social Insurance Premiums	Endowment insurance
November 2001	Notice of the State Council on the Opinions of the Ministry of Public Security on Promoting the Reform of the Household Registration Management System in Small Towns	Household registration system
January 2003	Notice of the General Office of the State Council on Proper Management and Services for Farmers' Employment in Urban Areas	Employment service
April 2003	Regulations of the State Council on Work-related Injury Insurances	Work-related Injury Insurance
September 2003	Notice of the General Office of the State Council on Forwarding Opinions of the Ministry of Education and Other Departments concerning Compulsory Education for Children of Rural Migrant Workers	Children's education
September 2003	National Training Program of the Ministry of Agriculture and Other Five Departments for Rural Migrant Workers from 2003 to 2010	Employment training
November 2003	Notice of the General Office of the State Council on Effectively Solving Default on Construction Costs	Remuneration issue

(continued)

Table 2.1 (continued)

Release time	Title	Policy highlights
January 2004	Opinions of the Central Committee of the CPC and State Council Concerning Several Policies on Promoting the Increase of Farmers' Income	Increase of incomes
November 2005	Circular of the State Council on Further Intensifying Employment and Reemployment	Employment service
February 2006	Several Opinions of the State Council on Settling Issues on Rural Migrant Workers	Social security
2006	Notice of the Ministry of Labor on Special Expansion of Rural Migrant Workers' Participation in Medical Insurance Program	Medical insurance
2007	Notice of the Ministry of Labor and Social Security on Issuing the Key Points of Labor and Social Security Work in 2007	Social security
December 2007	Guidance on Improving the Living Conditions of Rural Migrant Workers	Housing
April 2010	Urgent Notice of the General Office of the State Council on Effectively Solving the Problem of Wage Arrears for Rural Migrant Workers in Enterprises	Wage issue

of the Ministry of Human Resources and Social Security, by 2009, the total number of rural workers in China was 230 million, including 145 million migrant workers.[6] The transfer of surplus rural labor force to cities has not only greatly stimulated economic production, but also created conditions for farmers to increase their incomes and has accelerated the course of poverty alleviation.

2.4 Labor Transfer and Training

In its anti-poverty campaign, China placed special emphasis on the role of human capital, making full use of it in poor areas, and organizing and mobilizing the transfer of surplus labor force in such regions to other places enjoying greater prosperity. At the same time, it has attached great importance to personnel training and large-scale cadre training. The Sunshine Project and the Rain-Dew Anti-poverty Campaign are the two major policies introduced for labor transfer and employment training.

[Sunshine Project] In order to strengthen training aspects for transfer of the rural labor force, achieve stable employment and increase farmers' income, six government departments, including the Ministry of Agriculture, have, since 2004. jointly

[6]Duan (2011).

organized the implementation of the "Sunshine Project for Transferring and Training Rural Labor Force" (hereinafter referred to as the Sunshine Project). This was first implemented in twenty-six provinces and autonomous regions such as Henan and Sichuan, as well as the Heilongjiang Farms and Land Reclamation Administration and the Xinjiang Production and Construction Corps. A total of 2.8 million people received training in 2005, and the special subsidy offered by the central government increased to RMB400 million.[7] The training project, thus closely supported by the central government in terms of finance, has played an important role in capacity building of the country's western region, where a massive surplus labor force was transferred over time to other places. This has had a profound impact on the improvement of the quality and skills of the poor people and greatly enhanced their prospects for long-term development.

[Rain-Dew Anti-poverty Campaign] In order to resolve the contradiction between supply and demand in the labor market, and realize the transfer of the surplus labor force in poor areas, the State Council Leading Group Office of Poverty Alleviation and Development issued the *Notice on Strengthening the Training for Transfer of Labor Force in Poor Areas* in August 2004, and began to implement the "Rain-Dew Anti-poverty Campaign" as a practical expression of this aspect. It was led by the government with social participation, launching vocational education, entrepreneurship training and agricultural practical technology training to help young and middle-aged farmers in poverty-stricken areas to solve their practical difficulties, especially those related to employment and entrepreneurship. By the end of 2010, the campaign had helped nearly five million young and middle-aged poor farmers and two-hundred thousand demobilized PLA soldiers in poor areas to find jobs through vocational skills training, and ensured that each poor farmer household possessed at least one laborer mastering one or more agricultural production technologies with certain technological content. Its implementation marks the entry of China's poverty alleviation and development work from the stage of natural resource development to a new stage in which natural and human resources are simultaneously developed.

2.4.1 Adjusting Income Distribution to Narrow the Income Gap

2.5 Policy Concerning Individual Income Tax

The Chinese government introduced a new personal income tax policy in the 1980s. *The Individual Income Tax Law of the People's Republic of China* was released in 1980, but some specific taxation details were not introduced at that time. In September 1986, however, the released *Provisional Rules of the People's Republic of China on Individual Income Adjustment Tax* stipulated that the individual income adjustment

[7]Zhang (2007b).

tax should be collected uniformly, marking the beginning of an individual income tax policy.

With the rapid growth of individual incomes of urban residents, the threshold for individual income tax wasn't adjusted in a timely way, and more and more people needed to pay this. As of 2009, total individual income tax had reached RMB394.9 billion, an increase of 8.5 times from 1999.[8] At the same time, the growth rate of individual income tax exceeded that of urban residents' incomes.

At the initial stage of the individual income tax policy, since the threshold was much higher than the average income level of urban residents, and the proportion of people whose income reached the taxation standard was very low, the system failed to play its due role in regulating income distribution. In the case of the increasing individual income tax, due to tax avoidance by high-income groups and the individual tax characteristics (rather than the comprehensive tax levied by household), it failed to fully exert its role in regulating income distribution.[9] In order to reduce taxes for low-income groups and narrow the income gap, the threshold for individual income tax was raised to RMB3,500 in 2011.

2.6 Agricultural Tax and Rural Taxes and Fees

In the period of the planned economy, farmers suffered from a heavy tax burden, as they were forced to pay various kinds of fees. Especially in the 1990s, the taxes and fees borne by Chinese farmer households reached a fairly high level. According to a survey at this time, the tax and fee burden of a certain county amounted to a maximum of 28%.[10] Facing the problem of a mounting burden on farmers, the government began to conduct pilot agricultural tax reform in 2000, and the burden of taxes and fees in some places began to decline, falling to 2.8% in 2002. In 2006, the central government began exempting agricultural taxes nationwide, and abolished the right of local governments levying "three deductions" (for public reserve funds, public welfare funds and management fees) and the "five charges" (charges for rural education, family planning, militia training, rural road construction and subsidies to entitled groups). After nationwide exemption from agricultural tax was implemented, the burden of farmers was reduced by about RMB125 billion, averaging about RMB140 per farmer.[11] This helped increase the disposable income of farmers and mobilized their enthusiasm for production, thus injecting vitality into the economic and social development of rural areas.

---

[8] Li (2011).

[9] See Footnote 8.

[10] Chen Xiwen, Ed. *Research on Finance and Income Increase of Farmers in China's Counties and Towns*, p. 117.

[11] Huang Weijian. *The Impact of Abolishing Agricultural Tax on China's Economy and Society and the Next Policy Orientation,* www.cjyj.shufe.edu.cn, 2007–10–23.

Judged from the perspective of income distribution, rural tax and fee policies were fairly regressive, which led to a widening income gap. The rural tax and fee reduction policies adopted after 2006 effectively helped narrow the income gap and reduce poverty. According to estimates by Li Shi and others, taking 1995 as an example, if all agricultural taxes and fees were reduced, the income gap between urban and rural residents would be reduced from 2.47 times to 2.34 times.[12]

2.6.1 Strengthening the Construction of the Social Security Network and Focusing on Improving People's Livelihood

After the reform and opening up, the provision of education and medical services initially became extremely heavily dependent on market-based means, resulting in growth in the poverty phenomena caused by rising costs in these two sectors. Since the beginning of the 21st century, with the gradual establishment of the compulsory education and medical security system, this phenomenon was effectively alleviated.

2.7 Comprehensive Popularization of Compulsory Education

Successful reforms in education were mainly reflected in the comprehensive popularization of nine-year compulsory education with guaranteed funding, increasing support for rural compulsory education. In July 1986, the *Compulsory Education Law of the People's Republic of China* came into force, marking the full establishment of this system in China. In the 1990s, China further set the goal of "basically popularizing nine-year compulsory education and basically eliminating illiteracy among young and middle-aged people".

In order to narrow the development gap between urban and rural areas in China, the government increased its financial support for rural compulsory education. In 2005, the "two exemptions and one subsidy" (waive tuition and miscellaneous fees, supply free textbooks, and grant living allowances for boarders from financially disadvantaged families) policy was implemented for students from rural poor families, and boarders were gradually provided with living subsidies during their study at primary and middle school. The "two exemptions and one subsidy" policy was fully implemented between 2005 and 2007, and a total of RMB22.7 billion was allocated from State finances.[13]

[12]Li (2011).

[13]Zhang (2011).

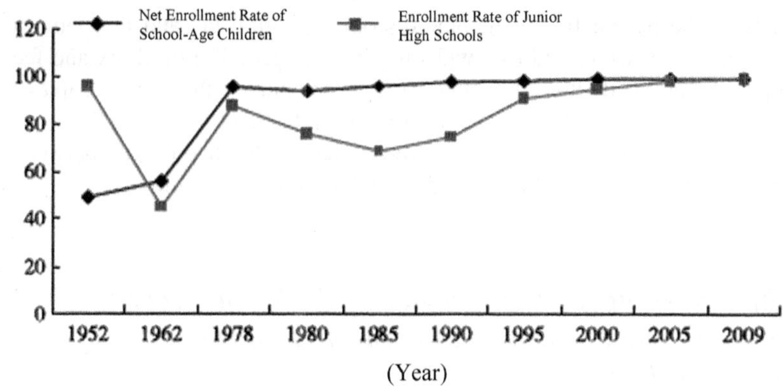

Fig. 2.1 Net enrollment rate of school-age children and enrollment rate of junior high schools. Source: *Compendium of Statistics 1949–2008* (2010)

Rural compulsory education was gradually integrated into the scope of public financial security in 2005, and a new mechanism for ensuring the necessary spending was established, with the central and local governments sharing the cost and implementation according to programs on a proportional basis. From 2006, all local governments undertook full school funding, providing free compulsory education in a real sense in the rural areas.

The policy played a key role in improving the level of education for all. In 2003, this increased from 4.3 years per capita before 1985 to 8.1 years per capita; by the end of 2010, all the 2,856 counties (cities, districts) nationwide fulfilled the goal of "basically popularizing nine-year compulsory education and basically eliminating illiteracy among young and middle-aged people", covering the entire population[14]; the net enrollment rate of primary school-age children reached 99.70% (the rate for boys and girls was 99.68% and 99.73%, respectively), the gross enrollment rate of junior high school was 100.1% (see Fig. 2.1), and the junior high school graduates' enrollment rate stood at 87.5%.[15]

Outstanding achievements were made in improving the compulsory education penetration rate and reducing illiteracy, greatly turning China's heavy population burden into a human resource advantage. Meanwhile, the subsidy policy for rural compulsory education played a positive role in improving the quality of life for the poor and reducing the gap between urban and rural development.

[14]Ministry of Education. *Statistical Communique on National Education Development in 2010*, http://www.chsi.com.cn/jyzx/201107/20110706/219482079.html.

[15]See Footnote 14.

2.8 Improving Medical and Healthcare Facilities and Healthcare Services

Reform of the medical system began in the 1980s, and it became market-oriented in the 1990s. Systemic reform in cities focused on the social basic medical insurance system, with pilot work beginning in 1994. In 1998, the *Decision on Establishing the Urban Employees' Basic Medical Insurance System* was released, marking its formal establishment. The social basic medical insurance system covered all urban employees, combining socially pooled funds with personal contributions. A series of policies were also introduced, including separation of prescribing and dispensing, bidding for medicine purchase, and classified management of medical institutions. After 2000, the government began to further deepen reform to promote fairness in medical security and provision of services. In rural areas, medical and healthcare conditions had been lagging behind. However, in 2003, a new type of rural cooperative medical system was launched, with government investment as the mainstay and farmers' voluntary participation. The purpose was to solve the problems among farmers that reduced to or returned to poverty because of illness, and ensure equality and fairness in service provision. From 2004 to 2005, the government successively introduced urban and rural medical assistance systems to help vulnerable groups to alleviate the medical burden.

Medical and healthcare facilities and services were much improved. The central and local governments raised funds through multiple channels to intensify institutional construction and further improve the rural three-level medical and healthcare system and the urban community healthcare system. A total of RMB40 billion in special funds was allocated by the central government to build 1,877 county-level hospitals, 5,169 central healthcare centers, 11,250 village clinics and 2,382 community healthcare centers.[16] At the same time, urban community healthcare resources were enriched by a variety of means, such as transforming the grassroots healthcare institutions and attracting participation of social forces.

With the reform of medical system and the gradual improvement of the grassroots medical and healthcare system, the masses had been able to obtain convenient and effective medical and healthcare services. As of the end of April 2011, there were 941,000 medical and healthcare institutions nationwide. At the grassroots, there were 33,000 community healthcare centers, 38,000 township hospitals, 650,000 village clinics and 175,000 clinics.[17] In 2010, the number of visits at urban community healthcare institutions, township health centers and village clinics reached 3.02 billion, accounting for 51.7% of the national total.[18]

---

[16]Zhang (2011).

[17]Ministry of Health. *National Medical Services in April 2011*, http://www.moh.gov.cn/publicfiles/business/htmlfiles/mohwsbwstjxxzx/s7967/201106/52031.htm.

[18]For details about China, please refer to Li and Luo (2011), Introduction to Overview: Income Inequality and Position in China, 2002–7, CBI working paper 2011–10, Department of economics, University of Western Ontario, Canada.

The improvement of the medical service system as well as medical institutions and facilities played an important role in improving the health of urban and rural residents. The maternal mortality ratio decreased from 1,500 per 100,000 when the PRC was founded in 1949, to 30 per 100,000 in 2010 (see Fig. 2.2), and the infant mortality rate dropped from 200‰ before the founding of the PRC in 1949 to 13.1‰ in 2010 (see Fig. 2.3), both the best among developing countries. Per capita life expectancy increased from thirty-five years before the founding of the PRC to seventy-three

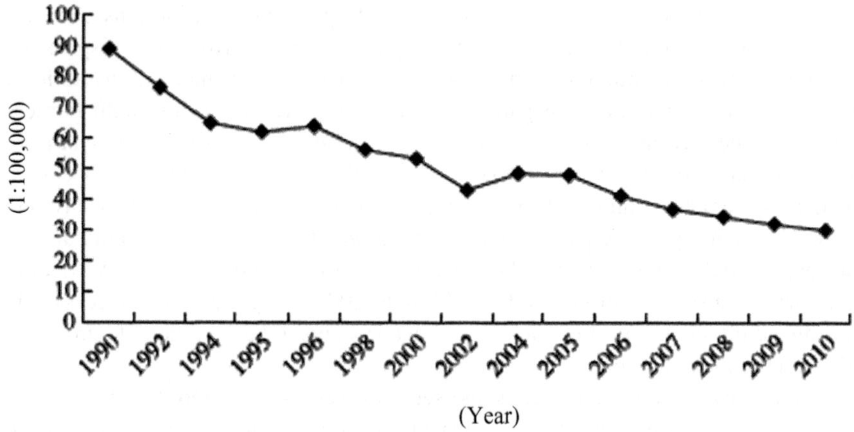

Fig. 2.2 Maternal mortality rate. Source: *China Health Statistical Digest 2010*

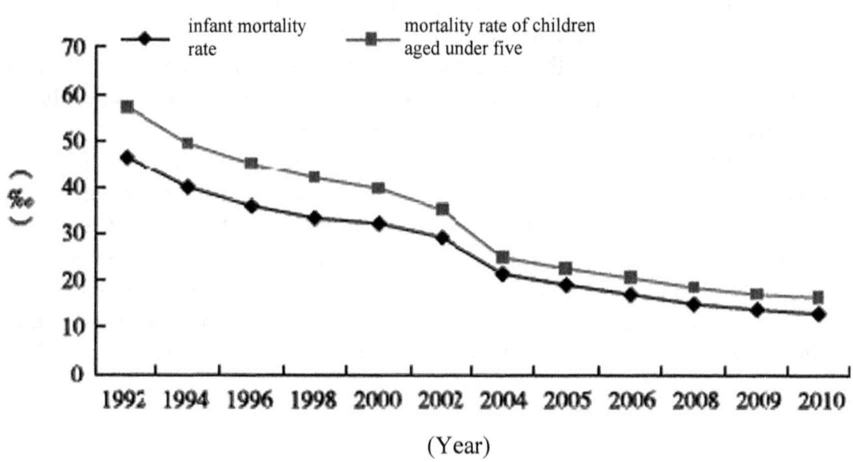

Fig. 2.3 Infant mortality rate and mortality rate of children under five. Source: *China Health Statistical Digest 2010*

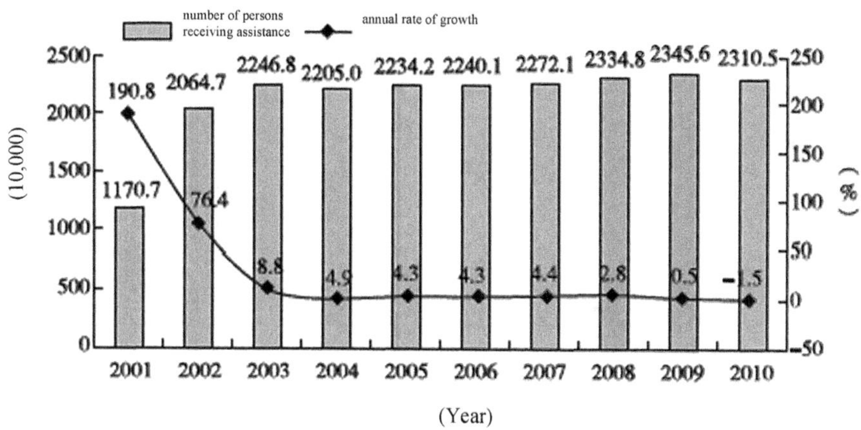

Fig. 2.4 Urban minimum living allowance. Source: *Statistical Report on Social Service Development in 2011*

years in 2010, and national health reached a relatively high level among developing countries.[19]

2.9 Establishing Urban and Rural Minimum Living Allowance System

The minimum living allowance system first started in urban areas. In 1993, Shanghai announced implementation of the minimum living allowance system across the city, marking the birth of the system in China. In 1997, the urban minimum living allowance system was formally established. The matching rural system was set up in 2007, and the minimum living allowance system of the whole society was formally formed.

By the end of 2010, there were 11.45 million urban households entitled to basic living allowances, encompassing 23.105 million people (see Fig. 2.4); governments at all levels spent RMB52.47 billion in subsistence allowances, of which 69.7% came from the central government. There were 25.287 million rural households entitled to basic living allowances, encompassing 52.14 million people (see Fig. 2.5). A total of RMB44.5 billion in rural subsistence allowances was distributed throughout that year, of which 60.4% was subsidized by the central government.[20]

As the essential social assistance arrangement, the minimum living allowance system achieved equal coverage in both urban and rural areas, and steadily sought to

---

[19]Ministry of Health. *2011 News Briefing on Maternal and Child Health Care and Community Health Work*, http://www.moh.gov.cn/publicfiles/business/htmlfiles/mohfybjysqwss/s7901/201104/51206.htm.

[20]Zhang (2011).

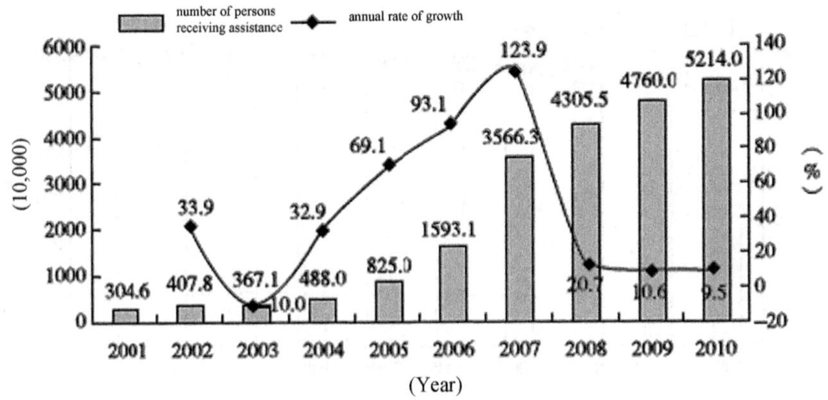

Fig. 2.5 Rural minimum living allowance. Source: *Statistical Report on Social Service Development in 2011*

ensure coverage of all those entitled to basic living allowances. It laid an institutional guarantee for a stable, lasting and effective solution to the problem of food and clothing for rural poor. In 2010, the national urban minimum living standard was RMB251.2 per person per month, and the per capita subsidy reached RMB189.[21] The national rural minimum living standard was RMB117 per person per month, and the monthly per capita subsidy was RMB74.[22]

2.10 Sustaining Inclusive Growth and Continuing Poverty Alleviation: Policy Suggestions

2.10.1 Promoting the Transition from High-Speed, Extensive Growth to Balanced Growth and Sustainable Development

The general requirement is to change the situation in which economic growth depends excessively on investment, exports, industrial growth and material resource consumption. Firstly, steps are being taken to reduce and stabilize the economic growth rate, use more development resources for economic and social structural transformation, cultivate structural growth momentum, support the adjustment of the demand structure, and realize transformation from an external demand-oriented, production-oriented structure to an internal demand-oriented, consumption-oriented structure. Secondly, there is a focus on supporting the adjustment of the industrial structure,

[21]Ministry of Civil Affairs. *Statistical Report on Social Service Development in 2011*, http://www.mca.gov.cn/article/zwgk/mzyw/201106/20110600161364.shtml.

[22]See Footnote 21.

using more resources for the development of the service industry, and realizing a transformation from an industry-oriented to a service-oriented approach. Thirdly, more efforts should be made to support the structural allocation and adjustment of the resource elements, using more development resources to promote new technologies, reduce material consumption, energy consumption and environmental costs, and finally transform economic growth from an extensive to an intensive one relying on scientific and technological progress.

2.10.2 Expanding Domestic Demand and Building a Consumer Society

Firstly, it is necessary to accelerate structural adjustment and institutional reform of national income distribution, and continue to reduce the share of government and enterprises in the distribution of national expenditure, to enable the incomes of residents, especially low- and middle-income earners, to grow at a rate faster than that of incomes of the government and enterprises and also faster than the increase among high-income groups. Secondly, there is an emphasis on making full use of public rights and public resources to create more opportunities for people to increase their incomes, reduce the number of poor people, and increase and expand the middle-income group, thus making it possible for the latter to become the main body of a future Chinese society and the mainstay for expanding domestic demand, stimulating social consumption and stabilizing the society.

2.10.3 Protecting the Rights and Interests of Workers and Improving Their Treatment

It is mainly to improve laws and regulations, especially laws geared to promote institutional changes allowing for farmers to settle in cities and towns as soon as possible, facilitate them to integrate into urban life, and increase the wages of the migrant workers and improve their social security benefits in cities.

2.10.4 Adjusting the Distribution Structure and Continuing to Narrow the Widening Income Gap

Regarding the adjustment of the relationship between different income groups, China lacks institutional arrangements and effective measures for adjustment among high-income earners. As a result, the rich pay less or even no taxes at all. Moreover, it has no long-term mechanism and effective policies for "expanding the middle-income group and increasing the incomes of low-income earners", so the middle- and low-income earners have narrow channels and fewer opportunities to increase their earnings. To this end, China needs to make two major adjustments in taxation to strengthen its function in income distribution and redistribution and its function of combating poverty. The first is to gradually reduce indirect taxes and increase direct taxes, and the second is to change the individual income tax from the current itemized tax system to a comprehensive tax. The former is levied on each item of income, while the latter on total household income. Collection of a comprehensive tax can help avoid the awkward situation that low-income people and poor people are also required to pay taxes, and strengthen the function of individual income tax in narrowing the income gap.

2.10.5 Continuing to Improve the Mechanism and System, and Striving to Expand Social Security Coverage and Raise the Treatment Levels

China's social security system covers birth, old age, illness, disability and unemployment, but is still difficult to provide effective protection for the low- and middle-income classes. This is mainly reflected in the following aspects: first, the institutional arrangements of social security for urban and rural areas, different regions and even groups are not uniform. The more backward areas, small and medium-sized cities (towns) and the marginalized segment enjoy lower social security benefits; yet, it is precisely the backward areas, small and medium-sized cities (towns) and farmers that most need social security. The lack of social security will inevitably curb the current consumption of these groups and force them to save for the future. Second, the social security coverage is too narrow. At present, the main institutional arrangements for basic endowment insurance, basic medical insurance and unemployment insurance are inconsistent for different groups and have too small coverage. Third, government support for social security investment is low and weak. In Western European and Nordic countries, 50% of finance is used for social security and social welfare expenditures; meanwhile, about 30% of U.S. finance is used for social security undertakings. However, the proportion of China's financial expenditure for social security in 2009 was less than 16.16%. Obviously, if the institutional and policy obstacles existing in social security are not resolved, it will be difficult for social security by itself to play its function in social redistribution and basic social security.

The full coverage of the social security system and the achievement of equality in public services will help regulate the income distribution relationship and contribute to poverty reduction. We must persist in deepening the reform to let the poor enjoy the benefits of social security but pay the least or even no price.

2.11 Insights and Lessons

In China, it didn't take a long time to practice inclusive growth from the proposition of this concept, but has always run through the process of China's reform, opening up and modernization. It is in line with the concepts of "scientific outlook on development", "harmonious development" and "harmonious society", becoming the country's guiding ideology for formulating development policies in different periods. This is of great significance for developing countries.

Firstly, the core concept of inclusive growth is to solve the question as to who benefits in the development process. The purpose of development is to allow more people to enjoy its fruits. Globally, coordinated and inclusive development among countries is conducive to the stability of global economic growth, and the achievements in economic globalization and economic development benefit all regions and all populations. Inclusive growth is not only useful for China, but also for the rest of the world.

Secondly, the concept of inclusive growth has always run through China's reform, opening up, and modernization. The Chinese government adopts corresponding countermeasures based on the characteristics of development at different stages.

Thirdly, it is necessary to continuously explore and improve the policy system of inclusive growth and advance the institutional improvement in an orderly manner.

Fourthly, due to different historical backgrounds and development characteristics, various countries should adopt policies and measures of inclusive growth suitable for their own development.

References

Chen, X. (2003). *Research on finance and income increase of farmers in China's counties and towns*. Shanxi Economic Publishing House.

Duan, Y. (2011). Review of migrant workers' social policy establishment and demands for their social policy. *Journal of Changchun University of Science and Technology (Social Science Edition), 24*(6).

Li, S (2011). *Poverty alleviation-based income distribution policy: China experience report.*

Ma, X. (2011). *Report on strategic choice of striding over the 'middle income trap'.*

Ministry of Education. *Statistical Communiqué on National Educational Development in 2010*, http://www.chsi.com.cn.

Ministry of Health. *National medical services in April 2011*, http://www.moh.gov.cn.

Ministry of Health. *2011 news briefing on maternal and child health care and community health work*, http://www.moh.gov.cn.

Ministry of Health. *China health statistical digest 2010*, http://www.moh.gov.cn.

Ministry of Civil Affairs. *Statistical report on the social services development in 2011*, http://www.mca.gov.cn/.

Su, M. (2011). *Finance and policy report for poverty alleviation and green growth.*

Zhang, L. (2007a). *China's development-oriented poverty alleviation process (1949–2005)*, China Financial and Economic Publishing House.

Zhang, L. (2007b). *The evolution of China's development-oriented poverty alleviation policy (1949–2005)*, China Financial and Economic Publishing House.

Zhang, X. (2011). *Social policies for poverty alleviation: A report on China's experience and choice of future strategy.*

Chapter 3
Income Distribution Policies as an Instrument for Promoting Inclusive Development: China's Experience

Shi Li

3.1 Inclusive Development and Income Gap: A Discussion About the Concepts

During the past four decades since the reform and opening up, China has experienced astonishing economic growth, especially in the most recent decade, with a GDP growth rate at times reaching over 10%. Such a rapid economic growth not only greatly has alleviated the poverty problem in both urban and rural areas, but also has contributed to a widening income gap. Under this situation, and seen from the perspective of inclusive development, the question arises as to how to assess China's development model. Regarding the income gap, the Chinese model being pursued does contain a deficiency in terms of inclusive development. However, when seen from the angle of poverty alleviation, the difference does not seem so great. The reason we have difficulty in making judgment is that we differ in understanding the concept of inclusive development. The main question is whether the model of inclusive development needs all social members to enjoy an equal share of the development fruits, and does it permit differences to emerge between members of different social groups for a certain period?

To find the solution to this thorny problem, there is the need to make a distinction between two kinds of inclusive development: absolute and relative standard. The absolute standard means that, in socio-economic development, all members of the society are eligible to enjoy the fruits of economic and social development, but different fruits are allowed to be offered to different social members. The relative standard means that all members of the society should enjoy the fruits of economic and social development on an equal footing, with no difference in benefits distribution. When seen from the viewpoint of changes in the income gap, the inclusive

S. Li (✉)
China Institute for Income Distribution at Beijing Normal University, Beijing, China
e-mail: lishi@bnu.edu.cn

C. Zuo et al. (eds.), *Inclusive Development and Poverty Reduction*, International Research on Poverty Reduction,
https://doi.org/10.1007/978-981-15-8446-6_3

development model under the absolute standard would be allowed to maintain or even widen the income gap. However, when it is treated under the relative standard, the income gap would have to be narrowed. Under the absolute standard, if the high-income group enjoys more development fruits than the low-income one, and the income gap continues to widen, it would be merely a low-level absolute standard. In another case, when the high- and low-income groups share equal amount of development fruits, it is a high-level absolute standard. Figure 3.1 shows the image descriptions of the three standards. Line Y_h represents income growth of the high-income group, and Line Y_l represents income growth of the low-income group. In the OP period, income growth is seen in both the high- and low-income groups, but the amount of growth of the former was higher than the latter, which means a widening income gap. This stage is called the stage of inclusive development of the low-level absolute standard. In the PW period, the income of the high-income group grows at the same pace as the low-income group, with no changes taking place to the income gap. This is a stage that belongs to the inclusive development of high-level absolute standard. Beginning with Point W, the income of the low-level group outpaces that of high-level group, with a continuing narrowing of the income gap. This is a period of inclusive development of the relative standard.

For any country, which inclusive development model should be followed depends largely on the initial conditions of its development gap. If the income gap in the initial conditions of a country is very small—such as the situation regard the income gap during the early stages of China's reform and opening up—and expanding the income gap is used as a necessary means to promote efficiency, it is necessary to implement an inclusive development model with a low-level absolute standard. If a country

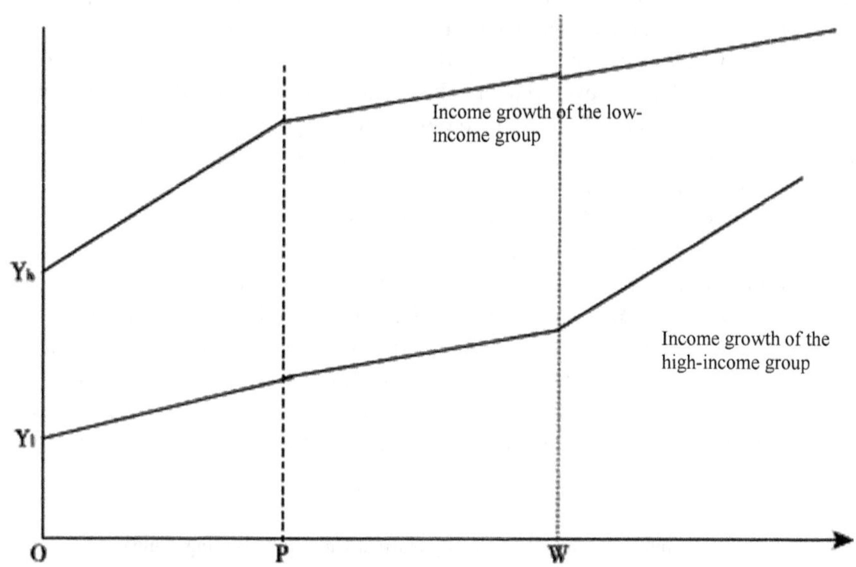

Fig. 3.1 Inclusive development of absolute standard and relative standard

possesses opposite initial conditions and its income gap is already large, such as China today, it is undesirable to follow the inclusive development model with low-level absolute standard; at the very least, the inclusive development model of the relative standard becomes a necessary choice, at least the inclusive development model of high-level absolute standard should be chosen. Now, the Chinese government has realized how difficult it is to adopt an inclusive development model of the relative standard, and thus persists in following one with a high-level absolute standard.[1]

3.2 Changes in Income Distribution and Poverty in China

Since its reform and opening up, China has witnessed many changes in its income distribution system and structure. It has changed from a country whose income distribution featured egalitarianism in distribution in the past to a country now with extremely big income inequality. From the global perspective, China now has become one of the few countries with extremely big income inequality. To review and assess China's development model in the past three decades or more, it's necessary to describe and explain the main characteristics of income inequality in that period.

The following are essential characteristics of the changes of China's residential income distribution since the reform and opening up program began.

First, the income gap expanded in an all-round way. To illustrate this characteristic, we might take a look at the income gap changes in urban and rural areas, and the country as a whole.

In the period from the late 1980s to the early 1990s, the Gini coefficient of residential income distribution in urban areas was about 0.23. Although the level of inequality was higher than the early stage of reform and opening up, it was still at a low level.[2] By 2002, the Gini coefficient of urban residents' income gap had reached 0.33 (Li and Yue 2004). At the same time, the income gap between the high-income and the low-income group had further expanded. In 2002, the richest people in urban areas, making up 5% of the population there, held 15% of the general income of all urban areas, with the richest 10% holding 28%. By comparison, the poorest 5% held only 1.2% of the general income, while the poorest 10% could only manage a 3% share. If we take equal proportion of the richest and the poorest group, it is not hard to ascertain that the average income of the richest 5% is about thirteen times of that

---

[1]The 12th Five-Year Plan formulated by the government only stipulated that efforts should be made to "curb the expansion of the income gap", and did not call for its absolute reduction.

[2]According to the National Bureau of Statistics, by the end of the 1980s, the income distribution inequality of urban residents was significantly higher than the early stage of reform, and the Gini coefficient had increased by 40–50% (Ren and Cheng 1996). Even if income in kind and various subsidies in kind are taken into account, this distributive inequality remains roughly the same. For example, the Gini coefficient of urban residents' monetary income in 1988 was estimated by the NBS to be 0.23; the Gini coefficient of individual disposable income (including monetary and physical income), as estimated by the Income Distribution Research Group of the Institute of Economics under the Chinese Academy of Social Sciences was also 0.23 (Zhao and Griffin 1994).

of the matching poorest 5%, and the average income of the richest 10% is about ten times of that of the poorest 10% (Li and Yue 2004). According to the latest statistics, in 2007, the Gini coefficient in the urban areas had increased to 0.36 (see Fig. 3.2).

In 2007, the Gini coefficient in rural areas was estimated at 0.38 (see Fig. 3.3). Results on the rural income gap differs between different research programs, but there are two common views: First, the existing rural income gap is much bigger than that of the early years of the reform and opening up program. According to research, the Gini coefficient of residential income distribution in rural areas was about 0.22 in 1978 (Zhao and Li 1997). That is to say, during the thirty years' economic transformation and development, the income gap of rural residents had expanded 68%. Second, from 1997 to 2007, income gap underwent both faster and slower expansion periods. According to the NBS, the Gini coefficient in rural areas increased from 0.32 in 1997 to 0.37 in 2002, that was a gain of five percentage points. This was a period of fast income gap expansion. In 2002, the richest 5% in rural areas held 18% of the general income, and the richest 10% commanded a share of 28%, while the poorest 5% held only 1% and the poorest 10% people managed a mere 2.5%. So, average income of the richest 5% was about eighteen times that of the poorest 5%, and the average income of the richest 10% was about eleven times that of the poorest 10% (Li and Yue 2004). From 2002 to 2007, the income gap in rural areas expanded slowly, with the Gini coefficient up only one percentage point (see Fig. 3.3).

With regard to the income gap and its changes nationwide, as the NBS rarely computes the Gini coefficient of samples drawn from the whole country, we can only discuss this according to the results of some research. According to the World Bank, in the early years of the 1980s, the Gini coefficient of the national income distribution was about 0.31 (Ravallion and Chen 2004). By the end of 1980s, according to the

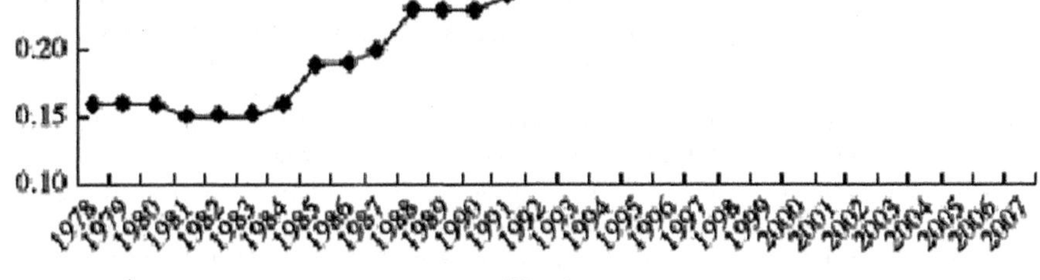

Fig. 3.2 Gini coefficient of individual income distribution in urban areas 1978–2007. *Source* China's annual income distribution report 2009, Chief editor Zhang Dongsheng

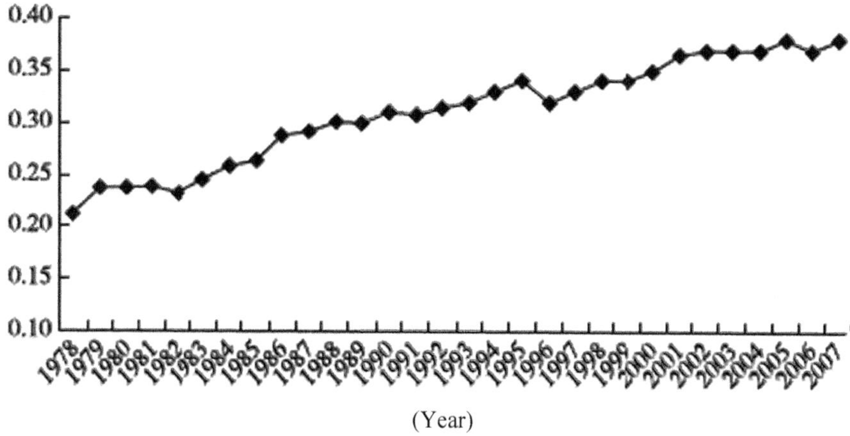

Fig. 3.3 Gini coefficient of individual income distribution in rural areas 1978–2007. *Source* China's annual income distribution report 2009, Chief editor Zhang Dongsheng

first household sample survey by the Research Group of China's Income Distribution, the national Gini coefficient was 0.382 (Eds, Zhao and Griffin 1993), with real term income and housing allowance of urban residence, and the imputed rent of rural residents counted as disposable personal income. Seen from the average incomes of the ten groups, the overall income share of the highest income group in 1988 was 7.3 times of that of the lowest income group (Khan et al. 1992). Investigations by the research group showed that, in 2002, the national Gini coefficient approached 0.46. If the income share of different income groups was brought together for comparison, the top 10% richest group controlled nearly 32% of total income, while the income of the poorest 10% accounted for about 1.7%. Thus, the average income of the richest 10% was nineteen times that of the poorest 10% (Li and Yue 2004). In 2007, the Research Group of China's Income Distribution surveyed the income of the same number of households in a way virtually matching the previous two sample surveys. The result showed that the Gini coefficient nationally was about 0.49, the richest 10% enjoying an average income twenty-three times that of the poorest 10% (Li et al. 2010).

Second, the income gap between the urban and rural areas is outstanding, with the changes of the residential income ratio in urban and rural areas reflecting the corresponding income gap changes. Since the 1990s, the ratio experienced the change of "rise-decline-rise again" (see Fig. 3.4). The income gap between urban and rural areas expanded from 1990 to 1994, with the income ratio rising from 2.2 times in 1990 to 2.6 times in 1994. After that, the income gap between urban and rural areas showed a narrowing trend, but this only lasted for three years, with the income ratio declining from 2.6 times in 1994 to 2.2 times in 1997—in other words, the income ratio declined to the same level as in 1990. However, beginning in 1998, the income ratio between urban and rural areas started to rise, from 2.2 times in 1997 to 2.5

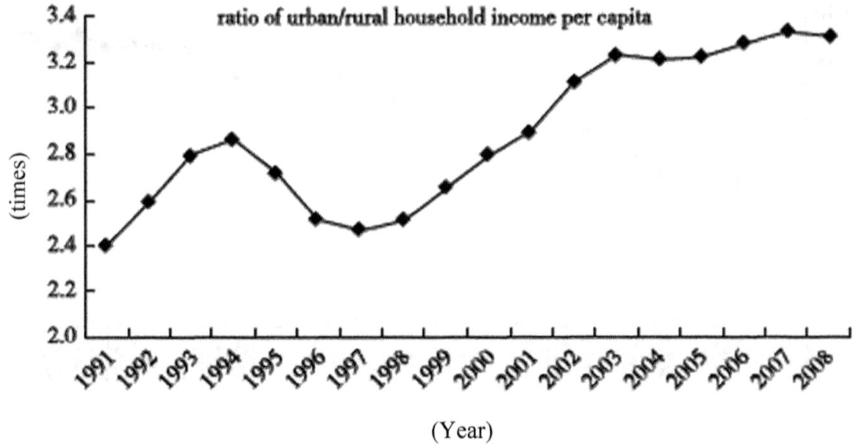

Fig. 3.4 Changes in the income gap between urban and rural areas in China, 1991–2008. *Note* Based on the data of per capita income of urban and rural residents in China Statistical Abstract 2009

times in 2000, and further to 3.23 times in 2003. In the next few years, the urban-rural income ratio fluctuated around that level. According to the NBS residential survey, the income ratio in urban and rural areas was 3.3:1 in 2009, then falling to 3.2:1 in 2010, and 3.1:1 in 2011.

If we divide the individual income gap in China into three parts—urban areas, rural areas and urban-rural areas, the ratio of income gap between the urban and rural areas in relation to the national income gap rose from 38 to 43% in the period of 1995–2002, an increase of five percentage points (Li and Yue 2004). This means more than 40% of the national income gap in 2002 came from the income gap between urban and rural areas, and this also showed the fast widening of the income gap between them was a major factor contributing to the widening of the income gap in China as a whole. According to the statistics available in 2007, the income gap between urban and rural areas in relation to the national income gap continued to rise, reaching about 48% (Li et al. 2010).

Third, there is still impressive income gap among different regions. Over a long period of time, China has been plagued by a protracted regional income gap caused by both historical reasons and new problems. Because of the existing big income gap between urban and rural areas, the regional gap is partly due to the difference of the urban and rural population structure among regions, and partly due to income differences between rural and urban areas. So far as the income gap among rural regions is concerned, there existed remarkable differences between various regions even in the early years of the reform and opening up. In late 1980s and early 1990s, following rural industrialization, a big imbalance emerged in terms of the income of rural residents, and the regional difference started to expand. However, in the late 1990s, when agricultural production remained stagnant and township businesses suffered from depression, there was no obvious expansion trend in rural areas. However,

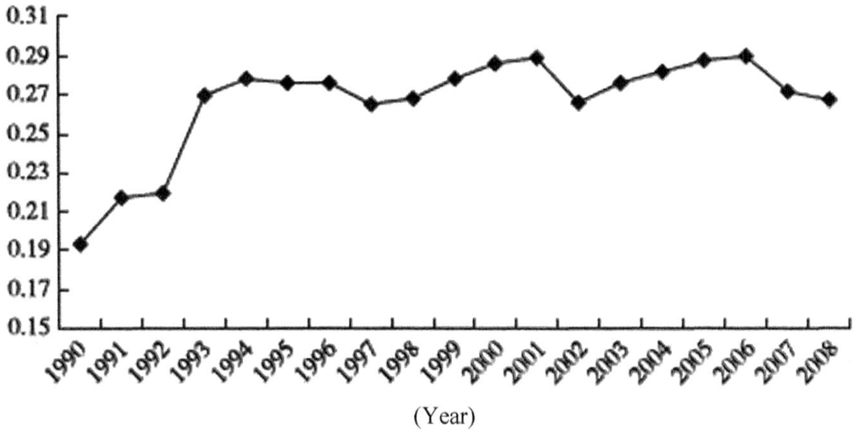

Fig. 3.5 Differences in per capita disposable income of urban residents between different provinces, 1990–2008. *Note* Based on the data of per capita disposable income of urban residents in *China Statistical Yearbook* of various years

what is different from the change of regional disparity in rural areas is that regional disparity of urban residents' income kept expanding. Figure 3.5 shows, in 1990–2003, the difference of per capita disposable income of urban residents in different provinces, measured by the coefficient of variation, kept expanding. This was especially notable in the early 1990s, with the coefficient of variation increasing from 0.192 in 1990 to 0.278 in 1994. Beginning in the mid-1990s, the coefficient of variation for differences in urban residential income among provinces fluctuated between 0.27 and 0.29, showing the expansion of the income gap in urban residential income among provinces started to slow down, although no shrinkage occurred.

Though in the past three decades, China has seen an expanding income gap, no polarization has occurred. The widening income gap is due to the income growth of the high-income group outpacing that of the low-income group. Moreover, the poverty-stricken population reduced significantly. From this perspective, China's development model is an inclusive one with low-level absolute standard.

From the changes taking place among the poverty-stricken population, we see the income of the poverty-stricken people and low-income people keeps growing. Figure 3.6 shows the changing trend of the rural poor in China since the 1980s. It is easy to see that whether it is based on the old poverty line or the new one,[3] the number of poor people is decreasing. According to the old poverty line, the number of rural poor decreased from 150 million in the early 1980s to sixteen million in 2007; and according to the new poverty line, the number of rural poor decreased from nearly one-hundred million to less than forty million over the past decade.

[3]In 2009, the rural poverty line was raised from RMB889 per person per day to RMB1196 per person per day. (see *Poverty Monitoring Report of Rural China 2010*, China Statistics Press).

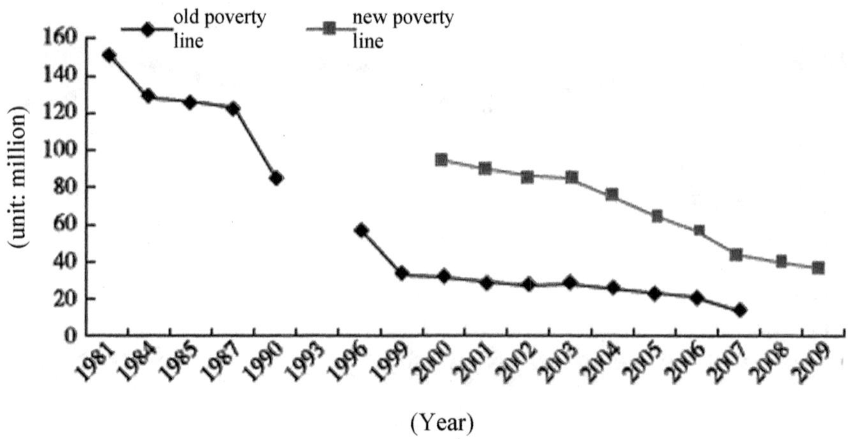

Fig. 3.6 Change trend of rural poor population in China. *Source* Poverty Monitoring Report of Rural China 2010, China Statistics Press

In 2011, the government again raised its poverty relief standard to take on more responsibilities on poverty alleviation, from RMB1360 per person to RMB2300 per person annually. Under the new poverty line, the rural poor population will increase to 130 million. This means that more rural people benefit from the government's poverty alleviation policy.

3.3 Assessing the Effects of China's Income Distribution Policy on Inclusive Development

In the era of planned economy, the Chinese government had extremely limited income distribution policy tools. It managed to narrow the income gap mainly by abolishing private economic sector, exercising strict control over the income distribution system in state-owned enterprises in urban areas, and adopting a collective distribution system under the People's Commune system in rural areas. At that time, the income distribution policy did not have much room to maneuver in playing its part because of low average income and small income gap. In the past decade or so, however, the Chinese government adopted a series of income distribution policies and made the following adjustments.

Table 3.1 Average tax (fee) rate of each income group of Chinese Farmers from 1988 to 2007

Income groups	1988	1995	2002	2007
Lowest percentile	7.5	13.9	6.2	0.3
Lowest quintile	6.5	12.0	5.4	0.3
Highest 20 quintile	4.1	3.4	1.7	0.3
Highest 10 percentile	3.8	3.0	1.5	0.4
Total	5.0	5.3	2.8	0.3

Source Calculated based on the results of CHIP data computation in 1988, 1995, 2002 and 2007

3.3.1 Agricultural Taxes and Rural Taxes and Fees Reform

In the era of planned economy, though the income of urban residents was higher than that of the rural residents,[4] the former didn't have to pay individual income tax, while the rural residents had to pay agricultural and other taxes and fees. There were four fiscal burdens for farmers: agricultural tax, tax on agricultural specialties, domestic animal slaughtering tax and deed tax. In addition, farmers also had to pay fees for various items. The part of fees they were required to hand over were called the "three deductions" and "five charges". In many areas, this part of fees they had to pay were much higher than the agricultural tax. In addition, farmers often had to pay a large number of fees demanded by local governments. In the 1990s, the tax burden weighing down upon the Chinese farmers reached a very high level.[5]

To relieve the increasing burdens on farmers, the central government felt it had to urgently resolve this problem. In 2006, it began to exempt agricultural tax nationwide and, at the same time, abolish the local governments' right to charge for the "three deductions" and the "five charges". According to a household survey in 2007, the tax burden on rural families became insignificant.

Table 3.1 shows changes in rural residents' tax burden from 1988 to 2007. The average tax burden was 5% in 1988, but rose to 5.3% in 1995. Beginning in 2000, China carried out pilot rural tax reforms, so that the tax in some of the rural areas starting to decline, falling to 2.8% in 2002. Following the exemption of agricultural tax nationwide in 2006, the average tax burden of Chinese farmers had been reduced to 0.3% in 2007. Such a change reflects the general situation of farmers' tax burden during this period.

[4]In 1978, at the beginning of the reform and opening-up, the per capita income of urban residents was RMB343, while that of rural residents was RMB133 (see *China Statistical Abstract 2008*, page 101), the former was 2.6 times higher than that of the latter.

[5]The "County and Township Finance and Farmers' Income Increase" Research Group of the Development Research Center of the State Council conducted a survey of the existing farmers' burden in three agricultural counties, and found their per capita tax payments was 12% of average income in 1997, with the highest reaching 28% (see *A Study on the County and Township Finance and the Increase of Farmers' Income in China*, with Chen Xiwen as the chief editor, published by Shanxi Economics Press, 2003, p. 117).

Table 3.1 also shows the tax burdens of high-income and low-income rural residential groups. Obviously, in the sample three fiscal years of 1988, 1995 and 2002, the low-income rural residents bore a tax (fee) rate higher than the high-income group. In 1988, rural families in the lowest 10% income group faced a financial burden almost double that of the highest 10%. In 1995, the gap was more than four times. Though the average tax (fees) of rural families was reduced in 2002, this produced virtually no fundamental change between the low-income and high-income rural residential groups.

From the perspective of income distribution, the tax policy in the rural areas had a strong regressive nature. It was not conducive to narrowing the income gap; indeed, the gap had widened. First, it has widened the income gap in rural areas. Computed results showed the Gini coefficient of the post-tax (fee) income gap was bigger than that of the pre-tax, which was an especially notable feature in 1995. This indicated that the taxes (fees) led to bigger income gap in rural areas. Second, it has enlarged the income gap between urban and rural residents. In 1995, for example, the income difference was 2.47 times. If the agricultural tax was exempted, the income difference would drop to 2.34 times.[6]

As not only well-to-do farmers but also the poor farmers had to pay tax, the poor thus became even poorer, exerting serious impact on poverty in rural areas. In other words, this increased poverty in rural areas, finding expression in the fact that it further reduced the living standards of the poor. Thus, it became clear that the tax burden weighing down rural residents was actually worsening poverty in the rural areas, with increased poverty incidence and poorer living conditions. We conducted a simulation calculation with data from 1995 trying to forecast the situation with regard to poverty in rural areas should all kinds of taxes and fees be reduced or exempted. Our simulation calculation shows, according to the official poverty line, the actual rural poverty incidence in 1995 would be 7.4%; however, if all taxes and fees were reduced or exempted, the rate would come down to 3.9%. Thus, the number of poverty-stricken population in the rural areas would be reduced by 47% when all taxes and fees were reduced or exempted, and the poverty gap would drop by 44%. This shows the tax policies implemented in the rural areas constituted the major policy factor leading to serious poverty in the rural areas, and, at the same time, while the tax and fee exemption policy followed after 2006 not only helped narrow the income gap but also helped to reduce poverty.

From the perspective of inclusive development, the purpose for China to adopt its original tax and fee policy in rural areas was to increase government revenue, with no consideration paid to the negative effects in terms of a widening income gap and increasing poverty. Therefore, it goes against the basic principle of the inclusive development model. The tax reduction and exemption policy the Chinese government introduced later, to some extent, caters to the inclusive development.

---

[6]In 1995, the per capita disposable income of urban residents was RMB3893, and the per capita net income of rural residents was RMB1578 (see *China Statistical Yearbook 1996*, p. 238). In that year, the per capita tax they paid accounted for 5.3% of their net income, showing the impact on the income gap between urban and rural areas.

3.3.2 Individual Income Tax Policy

China has implemented an individual income tax policy for only less than thirty years. In the first two decades of its implementation, however, the minimum threshold for the tax calculation was much higher than the average income level of urban residents, so that only a small proportion of people could meet the requirement. Personal income tax did not play a role in regulating the income distribution. In the last ten years, however, the income of urban residents increased rapidly, but the starting point of individual tax failed to be readjusted. An increasing number of people thus needed to pay individual income tax. As a result, the growth of the individual income tax revenue exceeded the growth of the income of urban residents, and the total individual income tax revenue reached RMB483.7 billion in 2011, 9.4 times more than in 1999. However, the individual income tax revenue accounts for only a small proportion of government revenue—only 6.6% in 2010. This mainly comes from indirect taxes including, among others, value added tax, consumption tax and business tax.

Recent years have seen rapid growth in individual income tax revenue. However, this has failed to play a significant regulatory role in the income distribution of urban residents, mainly because the individual income tax in China was a single-stage tax (collected on single-item income), instead of comprehensive tax (collected based on family income and the number of family members). Another reason is that some high-income people could find many ways to evade individual income tax. Efforts were made to further analyze the distributive effects of the personal income tax system, in order to enable individual income tax to become more progressive, instead of regressive, so as to help narrow rather than widen the income gap. Based on a sample of 12,700 urban residential households in a survey made by the National Bureau of Statistics (NBS) in 2008, we calculated the taxes being paid by urban households and the tax rate (tax amount/income). The result showed that the individual income tax paid by urban households involved a very low tax rate and the absolute amount of tax payment. In 2008, the individual income tax paid by urban residents averaged RMB267, with the tax rate being less than 1%.[7] At the same time, we calculated the tax payment and tax rate involved in each of the 10 identifiable urban residential groups of different income levels, and the result is shown in Table 3.2. It's easy to determine that the tax rate is regressive to a certain extent, namely, the tax rate for high-income group is higher than that for the low-income group. It means that, at least, by 2008, the urban individual income tax had a positive, but limited, role to play in regulating income distribution. The ratio of per capita income between the highest and lowest income groups decreased from 9.48 times before tax to 9.29 times after tax.

[7]This result is out of tune with the national personal income tax figures. According to official financial statistics, in 2008, national personal income tax collection totaled RMB372.2 billion. According to household survey data, individual income tax paid by urban residents reached RMB162.1 billion, calculated on the basis of 607 million urban residents (from the population statistics of the National Bureau of Statistics). It is impossible for rural residents to pay the remaining RMB200 billion of personal income tax. Of course, even if all personal income taxes come from urban residents, the tax rate borne by them is only 3% of their income.

Table 3.2 Income tax burden of urban residents of 10 income groups in 2008

10 income groups	**1 (lowest)**	**2**	**3**	**4**	**5**
Per capita income (yuan)	5427.4	8423.9	10,665.9	12,711.6	14,830.6
Per capita tax payment (yuan)	0.2	1.8	5.8	8.7	18.2
Tax rate (%)	0.004	0.022	0.054	0.069	0.123
10 income groups	**6**	**7**	**8**	**9**	**10 (highest)**
Per capita income (yuan)	17,265.8	20,276.5	24,258.0	30,534.6	51,466.6
Per capita tax payment (yuan)	29.5	60.7	117.1	251.9	1059.2
Tax rate (%)	0.171	0.299	0.483	0.825	2.058

Source Calculated based on CHIP data computation in 2008

3.3.3 *Minimum Living Allowance System*

The Chinese government transfers benefits to low-income people through a very limited number of welfare programs. One of these is the minimum income guarantee system that the Chinese government has been implementing for ten years. It was originally implemented in urban areas, and later extended to rural areas. By the end of 2010, a total of 23.105 million urban residents and 52.14 million rural residents received the minimum amount of living expenses for subsistence, and the rural residents received the minimum income.[8] Chinese finance at various levels spent RMB52.47 billion on urban minimum living insurance, an increase of 8.8% over 2009; this includes 36.56 billion earmarked by the central finance, or 69.7% of the total. The lowest life guarantee funds are offered mainly to three kinds of people—the unemployed, elderly without a pension and juveniles—who make up 70% of the recipients of subsistence allowances.[9] In 2010, the national average standard of urban subsistence allowances was RMB251.2 per person per month, an increase of 10.3% compared to the previous year. In cities and towns, the monthly per capita subsidy level of urban minimum living allowances was RMB189, up 9.9% over the previous year.

Although the urban basic living insurance exerts insignificant impact on the income gap at present, it does have significant impact on poverty alleviation. If the basic living insurance level is taken as the poverty line, the CHIP 2007 urban household survey is used to measure changes in the poverty incidence rate, poverty gap and weighted poverty distance before and after the basic living insurance is applied. The results show the incidence of poverty has decreased by 42%. More importantly, the poverty gap and weighted poverty distance have decreased at an even larger rate, reaching 57% and 63%, respectively (Li and Yang 2009). This means the subsistence allowances not only help lift a considerable segment of cities out of poverty, ensuring

[8]http://www.mca.gov.cn/article/zwgk/mzyw/201106/20110600161364.shtml.

[9]See the *Statistical Report on the Social Services Development in 2010* of the Ministry of Civil Affairs (http://www.mca.gov.cn/article/zwgk/mzyw/201106/20110600161364.shtml).

income higher than the poverty line, but also improves the living standards of those who, even though failing to escape poverty, can still alleviate their poverty.

From this, we see that the urban minimum living allowance system is not only a kind of governmental income transfer policy, but also one with the nature of income redistribution. Its impact on income distribution plays a limited role in narrowing the income gap; however, it has played an impressive role in alleviating poverty. It is, therefore, a kind of effective income distribution policy favorable for poverty reduction.

Compared with the urban minimum living allowance system, the rural version was introduced a few years later, finally becoming widespread in various provinces in 2007. As shown in Table 3.3, in 2004, only eight provinces implemented the minimum living allowance system policy for rural residents, covering no more than five million recipients. In the next few years, however, more provinces followed suit and more groups were covered by the policy, and the level of security also increased year-on-year. For example, compared with 2007, in 2010, the number of people in rural areas covered by the minimum living allowance system increased by 46%, and the per capita minimum subsistence allowance was raised by 67%. Allowing for inflation in the rural areas, the actual range increased by upwards of 55%. Moreover, the per capita income of low-income households nearly doubled.

The coverage of the rural minimum living allowance system has expanded rapidly, but, due to the low level of security, it has had very limited effect on reducing the internal income gap in rural areas. There is no difference as to the effect of income redistribution among people covered by the minimum living allowance system in urban areas. So, what has been its effect on alleviating rural poverty? Exploiting the data of the 2008 rural poverty monitoring survey, we calculated the changes in FGT index before and after the low-income group and the non-low-income group

Table 3.3 Development of minimum living allowance system for rural areas

	Provinces covered (one)	Households living on minimum subsistence allowances (10,000 households)	People living on minimum subsistence allowances (10,000 people)	Coverage rate of basic living allowances (%)	Per capita minimum living standard (yuan/month)	Per capita compensation (yuan/month)
2004	8	236	488	0.64	–	–
2005	13	406	825	1.11	–	–
2006	23	772	1593	2.16	–	35
2007	31	1609	3566	4.90	70	39
2008	31	1982	4306	5.97	82	50
2009	31	2292	4760	6.61	101	68
2010	31	2529	5214	7.24	117	74

Source: *Statistical Report on the Development of Civil Affairs Undertakings* of various years, http://www.mca.gov.cn/article/zwgk/tjsj/

obtained a minimum income. Results show the low-income security policy helped lift more than 20% of the people enjoying minimum security out of poverty, and has also helped alleviate the poverty situation of the people who have not yet escaped from poverty.

3.3.4 Rural Policies Benefiting Farmers

Since the beginning of the 21st century, in order to better implement the strategy of balanced development, the central government introduced a series of policies and measures to benefit farmers.[10] Since these policies are targeted at rural areas, and benefit mostly low-income farmers, these policies, to some extent, have the effect of regulating income distribution and benefiting the development of the low-income group. For a long time, the price of China's agricultural products has been generally low. Coupled with decentralized land management and the small scale of production, this has kept the profit margin of agricultural production very low. Farmers earn little from growing and selling crops. In other words, farmers engaged in agricultural production, especially involving grains and cereal, have always belonged to the low-income or poor groups. However, according to some studies, farmers' incomes from agriculture being more evenly distributed, has inhibited the widening of the internal income gap in rural areas (Khan and Riskin 1998). Therefore, subsidies for agricultural production, including food subsidies and price subsidies for agricultural means of production, will allow those engaged in agricultural production and management to benefit from accelerated income growth, thereby reducing the rural internal income gap and reducing the risks for them to tumble into poverty. In order to implement these policies to the letter, the central government's investment in agricultural production soared from RMB167.1 billion in 2004 to about RMB1000 billion in 2011, a near sixfold increase, with an annual growth rate of nearly 30%.

It is also worth mentioning that the compensation for Grain for Green Program has been effective since 1999. Pilots for the program was first carried out in Shaanxi, Gansu and Sichuan provinces. In 2000, the program was adopted in thirteen provinces and autonomous regions, including Yunnan, Sichuan, Guizhou, Chongqing and Hubei in the upper reaches of the Yangtze River in western China, and Shaanxi, Gansu, Qinghai, Ningxia, Inner Mongolia, Shanxi, Henan, and Xinjiang in the upper and middle reaches of the Yellow River, involving 174 counties. In 2002, this project was fully launched across the country, spreading from twenty provinces (autonomous regions) in western China to twenty-five provinces, autonomous regions and municipalities under the direct jurisdiction of the central government nationwide, covering

[10]According to the way the farmers receive benefit, the government's preferential policies for farmers can be divided into two categories: one is the subsidy policies aimed at directly increasing farmers' income, mainly including subsidies directly for grain production, subsidies for purchasing superior crop varieties and agricultural machinery and tools; the other is the public service policies aimed at building farmers' social safety net, mainly including the new cooperative medical system and "two exemptions and one subsidy" for education, and rural minimum living allowance policy.

1897 counties. As the compensation standard rose gradually, this policy became increasingly popular with local farmers. Judging from regional distribution, the project has benefited farmers living in the mountainous and ethnic minority areas, whose income level had long been far lower than the national average. The Grain for Green Program has increased their incomes, which helps narrow the rural and regional income gap. At the same time, these people are living in areas with a high incidence of poverty. Direct Grain for Green subsidies will help alleviate poverty in these areas, and also boost their earning potential. Because those who are borderline poor are also strongly risk-averse, they lack the liquidity needed as a buffer against financial calamity, and are often reluctant to look for work outside their home town. For the poor, compensation they receive for enrolling in the Grain for Green Program is something of an emergency fund, whose availability makes them more willing to look for work, including in nonfarm sectors, elsewhere As a result, it has a certain effect on alleviating poverty in the areas covered by the project.

It should be stressed that these policies do contribute to farmers' incomes. As shown in Table 3.4, between 2005 and 2008, the proportion of transfer incomes of farmer households in poor counties increased by 50% in their net gains, and that for poor households among the farmer households rose by over 66%. In comparison, the transfer incomes of poor households occupy a higher proportion in their net incomes than that of non-poor households. For example, the former was 30% higher than the latter in 2008. The rapid growth of farmers' transferable incomes is mainly attributable to government policies aiming to benefit farmers, of which the most important forms of subsidies and relief in cash are such schemes as food subsidies and subsistence allowances.

Since it is difficult to collect information on various subsidies from household surveys, it is not realistic to make a quantitative estimation of the income distribution effects and poverty reduction effects of various subsidies based on such data. Here, we can only make some basic judgments on two kinds of effects (income distribution and poverty reduction) based on limited information. First of all, policies that benefit farmers will undoubtedly help narrow the rural internal income gap, or at the very least help curb the widening trend. According to some macro data, in the past ten years, the income gap in rural areas of China has gradually expanded, with the Gini coefficient increasing from 0.35 in 2000 to 0.38 in 2008 (Zhang 2010). The widening

Table 3.4 Proportion of transfer incomes of farmers in poor counties in their net incomes, 2005–2008 (unit: %)

Year	Proportion of transfer payment in net incomes		
	Samples	Samples of poor households	Samples of low-income households
2005	4.5	6.0	4.9
2006	5.0	9.4	6.1
2007	5.4	9.4	7.4
2008	6.8	101	

Source: *Poverty Monitoring Report of National Bureau of Statistics* of relative years

rate during this period was significantly lower than that in the previous decade.[11] Although there are many factors affecting any decline in the widening of the rural internal income gap, the various policies implemented by the central government to benefit farmers undoubtedly form an important reason.

3.3.5 Social Security

In the past few years, China is undergoing social security system reform. One of the reform goals is to establish a social security system that covers all citizens. Extensions of the social security system to the informal sectors in cities and towns, to rural migrant workers in cities and towns, and to rural residents are all worthy directions of the reform process. Income distribution and poverty reduction effects implied in China's social security system reform also deserve attention and research, but there are certain difficulties encountered in this regard. The reasons for this include the fact that social security forms a part of public policy, and is largely reflected in government or individual expenditures rather than the income of individuals or families. However, if the concept of income is extended as an indicator of the well-being of individuals or families, any social security program that contributes to this can be considered as part of their income. In other words, given equal household disposable income, the actual income (income measured in terms of well-being) of families with social security is higher than those than that of families not enjoying this benefit. In addition, we can further estimate the market value of social security for each family as a part of actual income, and come up with a figure that includes this aspect. By comparing real household income with traditional disposable household income, we can see the impact of social security on income distribution and poverty alleviation.

Thanks to the extension of the social security system in recent years, rural residents have gradually been included within the scope of social security, and employees in informal sectors in cities and towns, especially rural migrant workers, have also been covered by social security programs, which has adjusted the distribution relationship to a certain extent and helped narrow the income gap. As there is not much research in this area, we are not clear as to what extent it has narrowed the income gap between urban and rural areas, to what extent it has narrowed the internal income gap in the urban and rural areas respectively, and to what extent it has narrowed the national income gap. Nonetheless, it is clear that the establishment of a social security system covering all citizens in order to benefit more people and reduce the differences in social security levels among different groups will play a positive role in reducing income gaps and achieving social equity.

For China, it is worth mentioning the momentum of government efforts to improve the rural social security in recent years. So far, the new rural cooperative medical

[11] From 1990 to 1999, the Gini coefficient for rural areas registered an increase of about 5% points (see Zhang 2010).

system has basically covered the entire rural population. By the end of 2010, all the counties (cities and districts) with agricultural population had been covered by the system, with 836 million farmers participating in the program, accounting for about 95% of the total number of farmers, and a total of 1.1 billion people/time across the country had received the compensation.[12] In the past two years, the government has continuously increased the proportion of its financial investment and the share of reimbursed medical expenses, continuously increasing the actual benefits of farmers. It is of great significance in alleviating rural poverty, especially in the case of "poverty caused by the burden of medical expenses". The pilot reform of the new rural insurance (new rural endowment insurance) that began in 2010 has not yet shown its anti-poverty roles. After it was rolled out in all rural areas in 2012, its role in alleviating poverty, in particular the poverty of the rural elderly, will be of great significance. Because these social security programs are based on government subsidies, they can also be seen, to a large extent, as the government's income redistribution policy, or an income distribution policy aiming to promote inclusive development.

3.4 A Stronger Role for Income Distribution Policy in Inclusive Development

International experience shows China's income distribution and redistribution policies still need much improvement. This is mainly reflected in three aspects: first, incomplete policy system; second, poor coordination between policies; and third, unclear anti-poverty goals of these policies. From the perspective of inclusive development, China's income distribution policies also need to be improved. According to the concept of inclusive development of different standards provided by us earlier, China's economic and social development over the past thirty years still reflects an inclusive development model with low-level absolute standards. In the long run, such a model is unsustainable because it cannot guarantee all members of society can share the fruits of economic development on an equal footing, and excessive income disparities can lead to imbalance in economic development and social instability. Hence, economic and social development needs to shift from an inclusive development model with low-level absolute standards to a model with high-level absolute standards, and income distribution policies should become more conducive to promoting this shift.

Income distribution policies can be divided into direct and indirect ones. The former refers to the policy itself affects the income of different income groups to achieve positive changes in the income gap. If a direct income distribution policy leads to a narrowing of the income gap, it has a progressive function; if it causes a widening effect, its function is regressive. Indirect policies aim to change the

[12]Data source: *China Statistical Yearbook 2011* (Available http://www.stats.gov.cn/tjsj/ndsj/2011/indexch.htm).

income distribution patterns by changing the opportunities and channels for obtaining incomes. For example, employment policies help achieve the goal of full employment, while increasing employment has the effect of narrowing the income gap. Therefore, employment policy is also referred to as indirect income distribution policy.

Based on these considerations, this article proposes the following reform directions for income distribution policies, with particular emphasis on their role in promoting the inclusive development of Chinese society.

Firstly, China should regard achieving full employment as the most important content of its income distribution policies. Achieving full employment is also one of the main goals of the inclusive development model. To narrow the income gap or promote inclusive development, top policy priority should be given to expanding employment. A large number of studies show unemployment is one of the main factors leading to a widening income gap and increasing poverty. Therefore, expanding employment will undoubtedly help narrow the income gap and reduce poverty, especially for developing countries. For an economy like China with a huge population and a large labor force employed in informal sectors, achieving full employment is also one of the prerequisites for realizing inclusive development.

Secondly, major adjustments should be made in China's taxation to enhance its functions in income distribution and redistribution and also in anti-poverty. The first adjustment is to gradually reduce indirect taxes and increase direct taxes. Tax theory tells us that indirect taxes are levied on all people, and the tax rates for different income groups are the same. In other words, whoever consumes more pays more, and the poor also pay taxes at the same rate as the rich. Direct tax is levied on personal incomes and corporate incomes, and a progressive rate can be formulated according to the amount of income so as to enhance its role in regulating income distribution. Reduction of indirect taxes will help raise wages to a certain extent, ensure low-income earners' wages grow faster, and also play a role in alleviating poverty. For another, we should change individual income tax from the current itemized tax to a comprehensive tax. The former is levied on each item of income, while the latter is applied to total family income. Through the implementation of a comprehensive tax, we can prevent low-income people and poor people from paying taxes, and strengthen the function of personal income tax in narrowing the income gap.

Thirdly, China's relatively weak income distribution policy is also reflected in deficiencies in government transfer payment programs. Existing transfer payment programs, such as urban and rural minimum living allowance systems and social relief projects, are operating at a low level. The government should classify various types of vulnerable groups, especially those considered unemployable for various reasons, and formulate corresponding transfer payment programs according to the characteristics of various types of vulnerable groups. In addition to implementing minimum living allowance system for low-income people, it is also vital to develop targeted transfer payment programs for vulnerable groups such as those with a disability, orphans, people living with HIV/AIDS, children and elderly people in low-income families, and single-parent families. Experience in some countries has shown that subsidizing children is an effective policy to alleviate their poverty and prevent malnutrition. For China, it is unrealistic to implement a nationwide child subsidy system, but this does not mean that this policy should only be implemented in rural areas or rural poor areas. Instead, it can also be implemented in urban areas for low-income families. Similarly, the old-age subsidy policy is also an optional income transfer payment policy. China's long-term social endowment insurance is linked to employment in formal sectors, meaning a large part of the population does not have social endowment insurance. Those in this category include elderly people in rural areas as well as those with no employment experience in cities and towns, and people who have retired from the informal sectors. For such people, it is vital to offer old-age subsidies, and this is also conducive to poverty alleviation simply because they are often the most likely to fall into poverty.

Fourthly, the full coverage of the social security system and equality in public services will not only help regulate income distribution relations, but also boost poverty alleviation. This reform must be maintained; however, efforts should be made to ensure poor people enjoy the benefits of social security at the lowest price or for free. Take the new rural cooperative medical system (NRCMS) as an example. Although the government has continuously increased its capital investment in the past two years, the reimbursement ratio for farmers is only around 50%, or lower in many places. Some low-income families still experience an excessively heavy burden of medical expenses. As a result, some farmers with economic difficulties due to illness refuse to seek medical treatment. Hence, it is advisable to implement different reimbursement ratios for different income groups. If farmers with lower incomes enjoy higher reimbursement ratios, it will make it possible for the NRCMS to play a better role in anti-poverty work. The same problem also exists with regard to the pension subsidies in some places. In the issuance of pensions, no consideration is given to family income status. Instead, a unitary standard is implemented. Therefore, when formulating the subsidy system for the elderly in the future, we should work out various pension subsidy standards according to the income level of the families containing elderly members. In this way, the pension subsidy will be more effective in dealing with poverty.

Fifthly, China's policies benefiting farmers will continue for a period of time, which is of positive significance for reducing the urban-rural income gap and alleviating rural poverty. At the same time, continuous improvement should be made in the course of implementing the policy. One of the important improvements is to increase its role in alleviating poverty. Direct subsidies to grain producers are now relatively uniform across the country, with no difference between developed and poor areas. Why not set different standards? For backward areas, especially those where poverty is rife, we can consider raising the standard of food subsidies, so that farmers, especially those on low incomes, can benefit more. It should be said that it is feasible to adopt different food subsidy standards in different regions according to their income levels, and it will not bring any foreseeable side effects. Moreover, the role of the policy in alleviating poverty will be significantly strengthened. For other agricultural subsidies, it is also necessary to consider different subsidy standards by region from this perspective.

Sixthly, while striving to achieve the goal of equality in public services, we must consider giving more compensation to poor areas and the poor. The policy proposition of equality in public services is of positive significance, attempting to modify the discriminatory public service policies implemented in the past for a long time. However, due to the long-term effects of discriminatory policies, some discriminated groups such as farmers and rural migrants lag far behind the general level of the society in terms of human capital and wealth accumulation. Even if the goal of equality is achieved, it will still be difficult for these groups to catch up with those who have been receiving preferential public services for a long time, and they are more likely to fall into poverty than other groups. Therefore, at the beginning of policy adjustment, it is absolutely necessary to provide more public services to these groups. Only in this way can the differences in development opportunities for different groups be eliminated as quickly as possible, and the vulnerable people be lifted out of poverty as soon as possible. One of the most prominent examples in this regard is the development of basic education in underdeveloped areas. Although nine-year compulsory education has basically been popularized in rural areas, differences in education quality is worrying. If the problem of low-quality rural compulsory education cannot be fundamentally changed, the problem of poverty in China will persist, and the poverty will "transfer" from rural to urban areas with the migration of the rural population. To improve the quality of rural compulsory education and reduce the difference of the education quality between rural and urban areas, the government should provide more support and make greater investment, and more quality education resources should be transferred to rural areas, backward and poor ones.

In short, from the perspective of inclusive development, China still has much room for development in reforming its income distribution system and improving its income distribution policy system. By supporting China's inclusive development model through implementing income distribution policies, we can achieve a higher economic growth rate, provide more equal employment opportunities, create a fairer public resource-sharing mechanism, and a more harmonious and stable social environment.

References

Chen, X. (Ed.). (2003). *Research on finance and income increase of farmers in China's Counties and Towns*. Shanxi: Shanxi Economic Publishing House.

China Development Research Foundation. (2007). *China development report 2007: Eradicating poverty in development*. China Development Press.

Deng, Q., & Li, S. (2010). Evaluation of rural social security progress and its poverty reduction effect: Taking minimum living allowance system as an example, a background report prepared for the "evaluation report on the implementation effect of the outline for development-oriented poverty alleviation for China's rural areas (2001–2010).

Gustafsson, B., Li, S., & Sicular, T. (2008). *Income inequality and public policy in China*. Cambridge: Cambridge University Press.

Khan, A., & Riskin, C. (1998). Income and inequality in China: Composition, distribution and growth of household income, 1988 to 1995. *China Quarterly, 154.*

Li, S. (2001–2010). *Evaluation report on the implementation effect of the outline for development-oriented poverty alleviation for China's Rural Areas (2001–2010).*

Li, S., & Chuliang, L. (2007). Re-estimation of China's urban-rural income gap. *Journal of Peking University, o.2.*

Li, S., Chuliang, L., & Sicular, T. (2010). *Changes in income inequality in China, 2002–2007.* Paper presented in the Workshop of Income Inequality in China, Beijing, May 21–22, 2010.

Li, S., Sato, H., & Sicular, T. (2013). *Rising inequality in China: Challenge to a harmonious society.* Cambridge: Cambridge University Press.

Li, S., & Yang, S. (2009). The impact of China's urban minimum living allowance policy on income distribution and poverty. *Chinese Journal of Population Science, 5*, 19.

Li, X., Zhang, K., & Tang, L. (2001–2010). *General policies that benefit farmers and evaluation of its poverty reduction effects.* A background report prepared for the Evaluation Report on the Implementation Effect of the Outline for Development-oriented Poverty Alleviation for China's Rural Areas (2001–2010).

National Bureau of Statistics. (2009). *Poverty monitoring report of rural China 2009.* China: China Statistics Press.

Ravallion, M., & Chen, S. (2004). China's (uneven) progress against poverty. World Bank, June 16, 2004.

Sato, H., Li S., & Yue, X. (2006). The redistribution effect of rural taxes in China. *China Journal of Economics.*

Sicular, T., Ximing, Y., Gustafsson, B., & Li, S. (2008). *The urban-rural gap and income inequality in China.* Discussion paper.

Wu, G., Guan, B., & Tan, Q. (2008). Evaluation of the implementation effectiveness of national food subsidy policy and its impact on poverty alleviation in poor areas. *Poverty Monitoring Report of Rural China 2008.* Beijing: China Statistics Press.

Ximing, Y., Sicular, T., Li, S., & Gustafsson, B. (2005). *Explaining incomes and inequality in China.* Project Paper.

Zhang, D. (Ed.). (2010). *Annual report on income distribution of Chinese Residents.* Economic Science Press.

Chapter 4
Inclusive Development and Fiscal Policy

Ming Su

4.1 The Importance of Inclusive Development and the Function of Government Spending

4.1.1 The Need for a Clear Understanding of What Inclusive Development Means

In recent years, the concepts of inclusive growth and inclusive development have been seriously debated by Chinese theoretical circles, producing a series of valuable ideas.

It is generally admitted that 'inclusive growth' was first put forward by the Asian Development Bank (ADB) in 2007. Its basic meaning is to share economic growth in a fair and reasonable way. It involves issues about equality and equity, including measurable standards and more intangible factors in related to these issues. Inclusive growth is defined as growth with equal opportunities in ADB's report titled *Poverty, Inequality and Inclusive Growth in Asia* published in June 2012. Its main policies include: creating productive employment and economic opportunities through rapid, effective and sustained economic growth; achieving equal opportunities through investing in talent capacity-building and creating a fair competitive environment; improving social security system, mitigating the impact from risks and shocks, and reducing dire poverty. Hence, inclusive growth aims to create economic opportunities and benefit all.

This paper is a background report for the *Global Poverty Reduction and Development Forum—Inclusive Development and Poverty Reduction* held by the Chinese government on October 17, 2012.

M. Su (✉)
Research Institute for Fiscal Science, Ministry of Finance, Beijing, China
e-mail: gaoj@ssap.cn

C. Zuo et al. (eds.), *Inclusive Development and Poverty Reduction*,
International Research on Poverty Reduction,
https://doi.org/10.1007/978-981-15-8446-6_4

The World Bank (WB) introduced the concept of inclusive development in 2008. That year, WB released *Growth Report: Strategies for Sustained Growth and Inclusive Development*, which clearly stated that "inclusive development" means to seek coordinated, stable and sustained development of both society and economy; to provide equal opportunities of free development for all and to allow more people to enjoy the fruits of reform and development through a standardized and stable institutional arrangement; to protect groups with special difficulties in many ways through preferential government policies and investments and to strengthen the capacity-building of small and medium-sized enterprises and individuals; to maintain balance amid economic growth, and to attach great importance to social stability.

Obviously, there is no substantive difference between the above definitions of inclusive growth and inclusive development. Both inclusive growth and inclusive development stress equality and equity, emphasize economic development results that can cover all groups, focus on development and improvement of people's livelihood, emphasize enhancing the income and welfare level of workers, especially the poor and the rural population, and focus on institutional innovation and policy improvement.

4.1.2 Fully Understanding Strategic Significance of Realizing Inclusive Development

Inclusive development has gone beyond general academic discussion to increasingly become an important governing thought of our Party and government. Hu Jintao, then General Secretary of the CPC Central Committee, elaborated on this important thought in 2009 and 2010, which was taken as a vital guiding principle for China's medium-and long-term sustainable development of economy and society in the future. The 12th Five-Year Plan is a period of strategic opportunity for building a moderately prosperous society in all respects. As transforming growth model remains a formidable task, it is imperative to build a new development paradigm aiming at inclusive development.

- Inclusive development is conducive to promoting balanced development between urban and rural areas and among regions. It is the essence and requirement of socialism to encourage some people and some areas to become rich first and then help those lagging behind to catch up with them, eventually realizing common prosperity. This policy has played a great role for China in breaking the shackles. The hindering problem facing China today is that, for varied reasons, this policy has not been fully implemented, resulting in an uneven development between urban and rural areas and among regions, a widening gap between the rich and the poor, and increasingly prominent social contradictions. Inclusive development is therefore advocated as a remedial measure. The purpose is to encourage industries to assist agriculture, and the cities to aid rural areas, thus making it possible for the rural surplus labor to move away from the countryside to work in secondary and tertiary industries elsewhere. Through this process, rural and urban residents can jointly share the fruits of reform. At the same time, China should promote inclusive development and continue to make efforts to implement the established strategies geared to the full-fledged development of in the western region, revitalize the northeast, energize the central region, strategies which will also play an important role in promoting regional coordinated development.

- Inclusive development is conducive for China to overcome the "middle-income trap". The "middle-income trap" refers to a state in which a country whose per capita income reaches the world's middle level lacks new growth momentum and faces economic stagnation due to failure of transforming its growth model. Basic features of such state include: economic growth slowdown or standstill, widening gap between the rich and the poor, frequent occurrence of corruption, excessive urbanization, shortage of social public services, failure to satisfy the society for employment, social turbulence, lack of belief, and fragile financial system. Cases in point include Latin American countries and Southeast Asian countries, which all suffer from this "trap" as they failed to properly deal with issues such as development strategies, income gap and foreign economic relations when they reached the middle-income status. In China, thanks to efforts made during forty-one years of reform and opening up, China now is witnessing high-speed economic growth and increasing income, with its per capita GDP reaching middle-income level of USD5000. China now is facing a huge risk of falling into the "middle-income trap". Inclusive development focuses on broader social justice on the basis of economic development, gives equal consideration to fairness and efficiency, ensures people's right to pursue growth, and highlights social welfare undertakings such as education, employment, health care and social governance. This will provide sustained power and basic guarantee for China to overcome the "middle-income trap" (Feng and Feng 2011).
- Inclusive development is important for pursuing and realizing social fairness and justice, which is the most inclusive and the core value of socialist construction. The social equity security system and mechanism aim to enable all people to have equal opportunities for development, and establish a social equity security system and mechanism with equal rights and opportunities, fair rules and reasonable distribution as the main content. It is conducive to eliminating the obstacles for people to participate in economic development and share development achievements, and form a good situation in which everyone participates in economic construction and shares development fruits. This, in essence, embodies social inclusiveness, social harmony and social fairness.

4.1.3 The Role of Government and Public Finance in Inclusive Development

To achieve inclusive development, the market and government need to work together. The World Bank's report entitled *The State in a Changing World* offers an empirical study on the economic development and government functions globally over the past one hundred years, and points out that the basic mission and tasks to be undertaken by a government under any country's modern economic conditions, whether it be a developed or developing country, include: first, establishing a foundation of law; second, maintaining a non-distortionary policy environment, including the stability of the macro-economy; third, investing in basic social services and infrastructure; fourth, protecting the vulnerable; and fifth, protecting the environment. It can be seen that the above definition of government functions and roles has, to a certain extent, reflected the objective requirements of the pursuit of inclusive development.

The Asian Development Bank has made a more specific and in-depth study on this issue, in its book entitled *Poverty, Inequality, and Inclusive Growth in Asia* published in 2012. The work is broken into four parts. One part is devoted to the study of policies and systems related to promoting inclusive growth. Its main points are as follows: First, governments must make efforts and invest resources to seek full employment of the local labor force. The report points out that employment is a basic human right, and prolonged unemployment and underemployment form a kind of social exclusion. Industrial policies play an important role in promoting investment to achieve full employment. In addition, the successful transformation of developing economies requires that private sector initiatives be brought into the framework of public action, a framework which encourages restructuring, diversification and technological progress. Second, the topic of access to basic services should be fully explored. Governments should focus on primary education, health care, water supply, public health and power supply and introduce preferential policies geared to improving and acquiring basic services (especially ones for communities where the poor live). These policies should include those enabling people to become rich enough to afford the services; help remove physical barriers; enhance understanding and awareness of required services and access channels; make more efforts to improve service quality; and intensify efforts to combat corruption. Third, governments should provide social security services to prevent extreme poverty. The report points out that social security is an essential element of inclusive growth, as it is a mechanism that ensures marginalized and vulnerable groups to participate in and benefit from inclusive growth. The solutions should include: strengthening the systemic and administrative capacity of the social security system so as to perform its core functions through better accounting, tighter financial control, human resources development, computerization and more information disclosure of stakeholders and partners. Governments should work to separate social security plans for the entire population from those for special groups with high risks so as to prevent scarce social security resources being diverted away from the most vulnerable groups who are in real need, so that the social security reform can match with other complementary reforms. Fourth, it highlights the importance of good governance and institutions as key policy issues for inclusive growth strategies. Research results show that the governance and system quality have strong and irrefutable correlation with growth and income level, especially in terms of the dimensions of political responsibility, democracy and corruption control. Therefore, when formulating development strategies, policymakers of developing countries in Asia could start with enhancing government work efficiency, improving regulatory quality and the rule of law, and controlling corruption.

Since the government plays a very important role in inclusive development, public finance, as a means of government macro-control, is bound to perform the duty and play a very important role in supporting and promoting inclusive development. First, public finance, through participating in the distribution and redistribution of national income, makes comprehensive use of taxation, expenditure, subsidies and other policy means to optimize the pattern of macro income distribution, adjust the difference of residents' incomes and wealth, and strengthen the support and protection for the vulnerable groups in the whole society. Second, by actively promoting the innovation of financial system, dynamically adjusting the transfer payment system and methods, and constantly improving the relationship between the central government, local governments and governments at and below the provincial level, public finance can lay the foundation for the vertical and horizontal balance of financial resources. Thus, relatively balanced development between urban and rural areas and among regions will be promoted to lay a sound financial foundation for economic development and basic public services in central and western regions, poverty-stricken areas and rural areas as a whole. Third, that public finance supports inclusive development not only produces a direct regulatory effect, but can also effectively exert indirect regulatory effect or guiding function of finance by means of fund distribution, and preferential fiscal and tax policies. Private capital, bank capital and foreign capital will be guided into the less developed regions and poverty-stricken areas, and fields related to "agriculture, rural areas and farmers". Wealthy class people offer assistance to the vulnerable groups by means of donation, charity, and others. This serves to better embody social inclusion and harmony.

4.2 Existing Fiscal Policy and Its Impact on Inclusive Development in China

Since the 11th Five-Year Plan (2006–2010), China has been enjoying fast economic development, with fiscal revenue and expenditure increasing year by year. In 2011, China's GDP increased to RMB47 trillion from RMB18.3 trillion in 2005, national fiscal revenue rose to RMB10.37 trillion from RMB3.16 trillion in 2005, and fiscal expenditure went up to RMB10.89 trillion from RMB3.39 trillion. With the increase of national fiscal and economic strength, China has adopted a series of major fiscal reforms and policy measures, which plays a key role in inclusive development and construction of social harmony.

4.2.1 Major Fiscal Policies and Effects in Recent Years

1. **Extending public finance to rural areas accelerated**

Issues relating to agriculture, rural areas, and farmers (hereinafter referred to as the "three rural issues") have always proved a bottleneck in the national process of modernization, and have to be resolved as the first step in pursuing inclusive development. It was first proposed at the 17th National Congress of the CPC in 2007 that the "three rural issues" had to be addressed as the top priority of Party work, and planning urban and rural development as a whole to be taken as the first of the "five overall plans", being the fundamental method of thoroughly implementing the Scientific Outlook on Development. With strengthened understanding of the need to solve the problems related to agriculture, rural areas and farmers livelihood, the government's financial support was increased, and the pace of public finance covering rural areas obviously accelerated. First, the financial policy system designed to resolve the 'three rural issues' were continuously improved. The longstanding agricultural tax was completely rescinded in 2006; farmers were given direct subsidies (those for grain production, subsidies for improved crop varieties, purchase of agricultural machinery and tools, and purchase of other means of production) from 2004; high priority was given to building roads, water facilities, power stations and other basic infrastructure; a basic rural public services system was established and continuously improved (including reform of the mechanism for securing rural compulsory education funding, comprehensive establishment of a new type of rural cooperative medical care system, implementation of new social endowment insurance system for rural residents, and establishment of a subsistence allowances system for rural residents); surplus rural workers were provided with pre-employment skill training to help them find new jobs away from agriculture; and the government award and subsidy system known as "One Case One Meeting" was introduced for rural public welfare undertakings. Second, financial investment in agriculture, rural areas and farmers was rapidly expanded. Central government funds allocated for this sector increased from RMB351.72 billion in 2006 to RMB1049.8 billion in 2011, with a total accumulated investment of RMB4012.2 billion in the six-year period representing an average annual growth rate of 24%. In 2011, national fiscal expenditure for agriculture, rural areas and farmers totaled RMB2934.2 billion, accounting for 26.9% of entire national fiscal expenditure, up 21.2% year-on-year. In 2012, the central government continued to increase this financial support, with central government allocations for them reaching RMB1228.66 billion, up 17.9% year-on-year. This included RMB472.42 billion spent on supporting agricultural production, RMB162.8 billion on the "four subsidies" for farmers, RMB531.39 billion on promoting education, healthcare and other social undertakings in rural areas, and RMB62.05 billion on agricultural product reserves and interest. Third, the integration and management of financial investment in agriculture, rural areas and farmers were constantly standardized. The introduction of financial policies and the increase of capital investment had combined to play a positive role in coordinately developing rural economy and society as well as increasing farmers' income.

2. **Concentrating financial resources to ensure and improve people's livelihood**

Ensuring and improving people's livelihood is not only related to the lives of the people, but also to the steady and rapid development of the national economy. Moreover, it is also the cornerstone of social stability. Since the 16th National Congress of the CPC in 2002, the Ministry of Finance, in accordance with the "Scientific Outlook on Development" and the principle of putting people first, has optimized the expenditure structure and concentrated fiscal revenue to ensure and improve people's livelihood, with focuses on the weak links of social undertakings, poverty-stricken areas, grass roots and vulnerable groups. Efforts have been made to build a long-term mechanism to ensure and enhance people's well-being so that our people can better share the fruits of reform and development. Between 2003 and 2007, accumulated national fiscal spending on education, social security and employment, health care, culture and sports reached RMB2.43 trillion, RMB1.95 trillion, RMB631.1 billion and RMB311.1 billion respectively, with an average annual growth rate of 18.6%, 14.9%, 24.4% and 16.5% respectively, up 1.26, 1.41, 1.27 and 1.3 times of the previous five years respectively. From 2008 to 2011, the scope of fiscal spending on improving people's standards of living was further expanded and financial support was strengthened. In 2011, national expenditure on education, health care, social security and employment, housing supply and culture, which are directly related to people's quality of life, totaled RMB3810.8 billion, 30.3% higher than the previous year; and aggregate expenditure on agriculture, water conservancy, public transportation, energy conservation and environmental protection, urban and rural community affairs, which are also closely related to people's lives, reached RMB3562.9 billion. In total, financial expenditure on people's livelihood in 2011 was RMB7373.7 billion, accounting for 67.7% of the total national expenditure. It could be said that China's increase mechanism of fiscal expenditure on people's livelihood now has been increasingly improved, and efforts China has made on improving livelihood are making constant progress. China today has achieved nine-year free compulsory education nationwide. China has also fully implemented assistance policies for students from poverty-stricken families studying in regular undergraduate institutions, higher and secondary vocational schools. In addition, it has comprehensively pushed construction of public health system and the basic pension schemes for rural and non-working urban residents. The framework of social security and employment system has been constantly improved. The low-rent housing security system has been basically established. All these effectively promote the construction of a harmonious socialist society (see Table 4.1).

3. **Transfer payments weighted toward underdeveloped areas in central and western regions**

In accordance with the goals of overall coordinated regional development and urban-rural coordinated development, and through continuous dynamic adjustments, the tax-sharing fiscal system and the corresponding transfer payment system, have, since the 16th National Congress of the CPC, gradually become the most important institutional guarantee and arrangement for improving capabilities of macroeconomic

Table 4.1 Social spending by the Central and Local Governments in 2006, 2009, 2010 (unit: RMB100 million)

Item	2006			2009			2010		
	National	Central	Local	National	Central	Local	National	Central	Local
Education	4780.41	295.23	4485.18	10,437.54	567.62	9869.92	12,550.02	720.96	11,829.06
Culture, sports, media	841.98	83.72	758.26	1393.07	154.75	1238.32	1542.70	150.13	1392.57
Social security employment	3031.58	246.81	2784.77	7606.68	454.37	7152.31	9130.62	450.30	8680.32
Medical and health work	1320.23	24.23	1296.00	3994.19	63.50	3930.69	4804.18	73.56	4730.62
Urban and rural community affairs	–	–	–	4933.34	3.91	4929.43	5987.38	10.09	5977.29
Housing security expenditure	–	–	–	1804.07	455.18	1348.89	2376.88	386.48	1990.40

regulation, promoting regional coordinated development and equalization of basic public service. All these have helped beef up fiscal capacity in the central and western regions and narrow the gap in basic public services between underdeveloped and developed areas in these regions. In recent years, efforts have also been made to intensify transfer payments while improving the distribution methods. After the reform of the tax-sharing system, national fiscal revenue is mainly used for transfer payments to governments at various levels, especially to the central and western regions. Between 1994 and 2011, transfer payments from the central government to local governments increased from RMB55 billion to RMB3488.1 billion, up 62.4 times, with an average annual growth rate of 28.4%; among them, the financial transfer payments increased from RMB18.9 billion to RMB1831.1 billion, with an average annual growth rate of 31.6%. About 90% of the transfer payments was used in the central and western regions. The proportion of transfer payments in local general budget expenditure increased from 13.6% in 1994 to 37.6% in 2011, with an average annual increase of about 1.8% age points. For example, in 2011, the central government's transfer payments to the central and western provinces averaged more than RMB100 billion, with Heilongjiang, Guangxi, Inner Mongolia and other places all exceeding RMB150 billion, and some even reaching RMB200 billion. This effectively promoted regional coordinated development and the equalization of basic public services. In terms of the total population, the per capita general budget income in 2007 was only thirty-one and thirty-three in the central and western regions if it was calculated as 100 in the eastern region. With the help of the central government's transfer payments, the per capita financial resources of the central and western regions rose to forty-seven and fifty-five respectively. By 2011, fiscal capacity gap among regions was further narrowed. Before the implementation of transfer payments, if the fiscal capacity of the eastern region was calculated as 100, the central region was only thirty-five, and the western region only about forty. After the implementation of transfer payments, the western region has reached ninety-seven, and the central region seventy-six. The balance of distribution has been greatly promoted, which greatly improved the per capita fiscal capacity among regions (see Table 4.2).

4. **Building the mechanism for ensuring basic fiscal capacity at the county level**

Financial departments at county and township levels are the grass-roots organizations of national finance as well as the functional departments of the county and township governments. They play an important role in pushing forward the coordinated development of local economy and society, strengthening the supply of rural public goods, and promoting social stability and harmony. Since 2005, the Ministry of Finance has adopted the policy of "three awards and one subsidy" for the counties and townships with financial difficulties; the plan is to mitigate their financial difficulties in three years. For this purpose, awards will be given to counties and townships with financial difficulties for efforts they have made to collect more tax revenue and to the governments at the provincial and municipal levels for efforts they have made to increase the transfer payments to the counties with financial difficulties. Awards will also be given to township governments and people for successful efforts they have made to streamline their institutions and personnel, and to major

Table 4.2 Changes in the scale of central to local transfer payments (unit: RMB100 million, %)

Year	Scale of central to local transfer payments	Financial transfer payments	Special transfer payments	Proportion of financial transfer payments in total transfer payments	Proportion of special transfer payment in total transfer payments
1994	550	189	361	34.36	65.64
1995	606	231	375	38.12	61.88
1996	774	285	489	36.82	63.18
1997	845	327	518	38.70	61.30
1998	1239	361	878	29.14	70.86
1999	1966	542	1424	27.57	72.43
2000	2459	846	1613	34.40	65.60
2001	3692	1492	2200	40.41	59.59
2002	4345	1944	2401	44.74	55.26
2003	4836	2238	2598	46.28	53.72
2004	6357	2934	3423	46.15	53.85
2005	7727	4198	3529	54.33	45.67
2006	9571	5159	4412	53.90	46.10
2007	13,991	7093	6898	50.70	49.30
2008	18,663	8694	9967	46.59	53.41
2009	23,677	11,317	12,359	47.80	52.20
2010	27,347	13,235	14,112	48.40	51.60
2011	34,881	18,311	16,569	52.49	47.51

grain-producing counties. Subsidies will also be provided to counties and townships that have properly mitigated their own financial difficulties. Between 2005 and 2007, the central government had been increasing the force of "three awards and one subsidy' policy year on year. Central investment made during this period totaled more than RMB70 billion, including RMB15 billion in 2005, RMB23.5 billion in 2006 and RMB33.5 billion in 2007. The implementation of this policy has played an important guiding role, mobilizing the enthusiasm of local governments to alleviate financial difficulties of counties and townships. Governments of various localities allocated a total of RMB80.8 billion as supporting funds; 791 counties with serious financial difficulties saw an increase of RMB129.8 billion in fiscal capacity, with an average increase of RMB164.1 million per county (county-level city). From 2005 to 2007, the number of counties with serious financial difficulties in China had been reduced from 791 to twenty-seven, and the financial difficulties that had plagued these counties and townships for many years had been greatly alleviated. Beginning in 2010, the central government has fully deployed establishment and improvement of the mechanism geared to ensure basic fiscal capacity at the county level. In 2010, the central government allocated RMB68.2 billion as awards and subsidies in a bid to strengthen financial support of counties in providing basic public services. In 2011, a total of RMB77.5 billion was allocated as awards and subsidies within the mechanism for ensuring basic fiscal capacity at the county level, up 13.6%. In 2012, the budgeted figure even exceeded RMB100 billion, reaching RMB107.5 billion, up 38.7%. The establishment of the central reward and subsidy mechanism, coupled by efforts made to guide and encourage local governments to adjust and improve the financial system below the provincial level, has increased the transfer payments of county-level finance. This serves to promote the development of county-level economy, strengthen the management of county-level financial revenue and expenditure, thereby effectively improving the county-level financial support, and greatly alleviating financial difficulties at the grassroots level.

5. **Vigorously supporting poverty alleviation and development**

From both the domestic and international perspectives, addressing the poverty issue has always been the top priority in all government work. It is an important part of achieving inclusive development and promoting social stability. It is also a key function of government finance. With rapid economic development in the past 30-odd years of reform and opening up, China has made persistent efforts to promote development-oriented poverty alleviation with great success, enjoying a high reputation internationally. Fiscal policy has played a crucial role in this regard. In 2001, the government released and implemented the *Outline for Development-oriented Poverty Alleviation for China's Rural Areas (2001–2010)* (hereinafter referred to as the Outline). In the past decade, the central and provincial governments have further increased their funding for poverty alleviation with more standardized fund management, thus greatly promoting overall national development. Firstly, financial investment in poverty alleviation has increased steadily. In the ten years in which the Outline has been implemented, the central government has invested more than RMB144 billion in special funds for poverty alleviation, registering an average annual growth of 9.7%, and local governments at all levels have also increased their own investment. More than RMB140 billion of loans have been channeled into poverty reduction through fiscal discounts. In 2010, the central and provincial fiscal budgets for poverty alleviation totaled RMB30.268 billion, an increase of 15.7% year-on-year. The central fiscal budget for this purpose hit RMB22.268 billion, a rise of 12.9%; provincial spending reached RMB8 billion, up 24.45%. Secondly, China makes investment in a centralized way and with a strong emphasis. Of the RMB21.288 billion of poverty alleviation funds allocated by the central government to provincial governments in 2010, RMB20.94 billion went to twenty-two provinces in the central and western regions, accounting for 98.37% of the total poverty alleviation funds; funding for the western region alone accounted for 66.5%. A total of RMB14.89 billion was invested in key poverty-stricken counties enjoying support from the national government, and RMB19.12 billion in poverty-stricken villages. These funds were used to finance programs undertaken to promote overall village

Table 4.3 Poor population and incidence of poverty in china and key poverty reduction counties

Year	Poverty standard (yuan)	Whole nation		Key poverty alleviation countries	
		Impoverished population (10,000 people)	Incidence of poverty (%)	Impoverished population (10,000 people)	Incidence of poverty (%)
2000	865	9422	10.2	–	–
2001	872	9030	9.8	–	–
2002	869	8645	9.2	4828	24.3
2003	882	8517	9.1	4706	23.7
2004	924	7587	8.0	4193	21.0
2005	944	6432	6.8	3611	18.0
2006	958	5698	6.0	3110	15.4
2007	1067	4320	4.6	2620	13.0
2008	1196	4007	4.2	2421	11.9
2009	1196	3597	3.8	2175	10.7
2010	1274	2688	2.8	1693	8.3

Source Rural housing sampling survey and rural poverty monitoring survey, National Bureau of Statistics

development, training for the transfer of rural laborers experiencing financial difficulties due to lack of work, and poverty alleviation through industrialization or migration. Thirdly, China has achieved considerable innovation in the related mechanisms, and improved the efficiency of capital use. Specific measures include pilot arrangement of mutual aid funds for poor villages, and guidance through finance discount, and performance evaluation. With their implementation, China has established a fiscal policy framework system for multi-channel poverty reduction, enhancing the poverty combating capabilities of the poorest areas, improving environment and conditions for development, and alleviating the outstanding difficulties faced by the poor in their production activities and daily life. From the end of 2000 to 2010, the rural poverty-stricken population fell from 94.22 million to 26.88 million, and the incidence of poverty declined from 10.2 to 2.8% (see Table 4.3).

4.2.2 Main Problems

Although the central government financial department adopted numerous reforms and policy measures to support inclusive development with significant results in the past over ten years, there are still many contradictions amid inclusive development and social harmony despite rapid national economic growth. The main contradictions are as follows.

1. **Income gap of the whole society tends to widen, and the problem of unfair distribution is to get worse**

First, society-wide income inequality. Internationally, the Gini coefficient is usually used to judge the degree of fairness of income distribution. This index ranges from zero to one. The lower the value, the more even the distribution of wealth among members of society, with 0.4 usually seen as the "warning line" in regard to the income distribution gap. The Gini coefficient of developed countries is 0.24 to 0.36. According to a World Bank report, China's Gini coefficient was about 0.17–0.18 in the 1960s and 0.21–0.27 in the 1980s. However, it crossed the warning line of 0.4 in 2000, and continued to increase year by year. Relevant data show that it was 0.382 in 1988, 0.445 in 1995, 0.454 in 2000, 0.458 in 2003, 0.465 in 2004, 0.47 in 2005, 0.47 in 2006, 0.48 in 2007, and 0.54 in 2010. According to UNDP statistics, China's poorest population, which currently accounts for 20% of total population, has access to only 4.7% of overall income or consumption, while the richest population, also 20% of the total, controls 50% of income or consumption. The ratio of the average income of the top 20% to the lowest 20% was 10.7 in China, compared to 8.4 in the United States, 4.5 in Russia, 4.9 in India, and 3.4 in Japan, which was the lowest. According to a World Bank report, 5% of the population in the United States controls 60% of total national wealth, while 1% of Chinese households control 41.4%. This means that, since the reform and opening up, China has changed from one of the countries with the most even income distribution among residents to one with a large income gap.

Second, there is a widening income gap between urban and rural areas. Since the reform and opening up program began, the incomes of both urban and rural residents have increased significantly, but the income gap has gradually widened from a low point in 1985. It was 1: 2.01 in 1990, 1: 2.72 in 1995, 1: 2.79 in 2000, 1: 3.22 in 2005, and 1: 3.23 in 2010 (see Table 4.4 for details).

Third, there is a widening income gap between regions. China's regional disparity declined to some extent in the 1980s, but has been rising ever since the 1990s. The overall regional disparity in China mainly comes from the gap between inland and coastal areas. As of 2009, the average annual income of urban households in the prosperous eastern region was RMB23,153.21, which was RMB7,613.82, 7630.18 and RMB7,310.57 higher than levels in the central, western and northeastern regions respectively. The average wage of urban employees in Jiangxi Province (RMB24,156), for example, was only 41.4% of that in Shanghai (RMB58,336).

Fourth, there is an income gap between industries. The latest data released by the Wage Research Institute at the Ministry of Human Resources and Social Security show the difference between the highest-income and lowest-income industries has expanded 15-fold, ranking first in the world. Among the three industries with the highest average wages, the per capita wage of the securities industry is RMB172,100, six times the national average; that of other financial industries has reached RMB87,670, 3.1 times the national average; and that of the aviation industry has stood at RMB75,800, 2.6 times greater than the national average. Workers in state-owned industries such as electric power, telecommunications, petroleum, finance,

Table 4.4 Disposable incomes of urban and rural households in China from 1978 to 2010

Year	Per capita disposable income of urban households		Per capita net income of rural households		Per capita income gap between urban and rural areas	Ratio of urban and rural per capita income (1 based on farmers' income)
	Absolute number (yuan)	Index (1978 = 100)	Absolute number (yuan)	Index (1978 = 100)		
1978	343.4	100.0	133.6	100.0	209.8	1:2.58
1980	477.6	127.0	191.3	139.0	286.3	1:2.50
1985	739.1	160.4	397.6	268.9	341.5	1:1.86
1990	1510.2	198.1	686.3	311.2	823.9	1:2.01
1995	4283.0	212.4	1577.7	383.6	2705.3	1:2.72
2000	6280.0	290.3	2253.4	483.4	4026.6	1:2.79
2005	10,493.0	383.7	3254.9	–	7238.1	1:3.22
2010	19,109.4	965.2	5919.0	954.4	13,190.0	1:3.23

insurance, water, electricity and gas supply, and tobacco account for less than 8% of the national total, but their total wages and extra-wage income are equivalent to 55% of the overall total. The phenomenon of "strong capital and weak labor" is very prominent.

2. **Insufficient supply of basic public services and uneven development**

The report to the 17th National Congress of the CPC put forward "improving the public finance system while working to ensure equal access to basic public services and establish development priority zones" as a top priority. It can be seen that ensuring equal access to public services has become an important part of the work to improve China's public fiscal system. In recent years, according to the central government's plan, it has actually increased investment in people's livelihood, and achieved remarkable results in providing basic public services. However, in general, the issues of insufficient supply of basic public services and imbalanced development remain prominent.

From the perspective of supply, the standards and scope of basic public services have been unclear for a long time, and there has been insufficient investment in public welfare services for a prolonged period. Historical debts are large, and the needs of the society can hardly be met.

From the perspective of urban and rural areas, public services in the latter seriously lag behind, with poor accessibility. In terms of compulsory education, in 2008, the per capita educational outlay of urban ordinary primary and junior high schools was 1.2 times and 1.3 times that of rural areas respectively, and the proportion of teachers with higher academic qualifications in urban ordinary middle schools was almost twice that of rural ones. With regard to health care, in 2008, the number of hospital beds per thousand people in cities was 4.22 times that in rural areas, and the number of health professionals per thousand people was 2.52 times that in rural areas. The infant mortality rate, mortality among children aged under five, and maternal mortality rate in rural areas were 2.8, 2.9 and 1.2 times those in cities, respectively.

From a regional perspective, the level of public services is positively related to that of economic development; however, the gap between different regions in terms of public services is greater than the economic level. In recent years, the coefficient of variation in per capita GDP between regions has gradually decreased, but that in public services is still large. In 2008, the coefficient of variation in per capita local education, social security and employment, and medical and healthcare expenditure was 0.529, much higher than the per capita disposable income of urban residents in the same period (0.267). In another example, the current highest provincial education expenditure for each primary school student is nearly ten times the lowest, and the difference of the financial subsidies for the new rural cooperative medical system between regions is more than four times. Such data reflect the huge gaps between regions.

In addition, the gap between different groups is also large, and the rights and interests in regards to basic public services for low-income families and socially vulnerable groups in urban and rural areas have not been fully guaranteed. In 2006, *Several Opinions on Settling Issues on Rural Migrant Workers* released by the State Council offered guidance on rural migrant workers' wages, employment, labor protection, social security, and reform of the household registration management system. Thanks to the implementation of these policies and measures, the overall situation of rural migrant workers greatly improved. However, compared with the resident population in urban areas, rural migrant workers still face a large gap in terms of wage income and basic public services. The coverage of basic social security is relatively low among rural migrant workers. In 2006, however, great progress was achieved in rural migrant workers' participation in the basic medical insurance program. A total of 23.67 million rural migrant workers participated in it, an increase of 18.78 million over the previous year. However, the proportion of rural migrant workers covered by the basic social security program is still low. According to survey data released by the Chinese Academy of Social Sciences, the current proportion of rural migrant workers participating in the endowment, unemployment, medical treatment and work-related injury insurance programs, and the mutual assistance and cooperation insurance program for female employees, is 33.7%, 10.3%, 21.6%, 31.8%, and 5.5% respectively, far lower than the level of their urban counterparts. The proportion of rural migrant workers who have been covered by corporate supplementary insurance, mutual assistance and cooperation insurance for employees, and commercial insurance is even lower, being 2.9%, 3.1% and 5.6% respectively. A survey by the National Bureau of Statistics shows that 74.81% of rural migrant workers have never been insured. The proportion of rural migrant workers who have endowment insurance, medical insurance, unemployment insurance or work-related injury insurance purchased by employers is only 11.89%, 12.61%, 8.41% and 23.09% respectively (*people.cn*, 2008).

In general, the central government has increased its financial supply to compulsory education, public health and basic medical services, basic social security, and public employment services in the past decade. Positive progress has been made in achieving equality in basic public services. However, due to low-level development of productive forces and relatively backward social construction, basic public services still face a number of outstanding problems, such as low level, large historical debts, poor coverage, insufficient investment and uneven financial input. From a closer look at the problems, we find they are caused by imperfect systems and mechanisms in basic public services. They include an inferior public financial security mechanism, a dual supply system with urban-rural division, fragmented and unreasonable distribution of basic public service resources, mismatch between the administrative and financial power of grass-roots governments, and lack of an effective evaluation and supervision mechanism. This reflects not only the contradiction of uncoordinated economic and social development, but also the construction of basic public service system lagging far behind need. Therefore, there is still a long way to go for China to truly form a complete system and achieve total equality. This points up to the fact that future tasks are fairly arduous and urgent, so great efforts are still needed.

It must be pointed out that the large gap in provision of basic public services between regions, between urban and rural areas, and among different social groups will become a major obstacle in China's current poverty alleviation efforts. Basic public services are scarce resources. Their distribution, if unfair, will restrict everyone in achieving their full abilities. In particular, the provision of basic public services, such as compulsory education, basic medical care and minimum living allowance, is not only related to improvement of laborers' quality but also has huge social benefits beyond the return on individual investment. It is the basic prerequisite to bring individual potential into full play and realize equal opportunities for individual participation. It is also an important factor affecting the income level of residents. An important reason for poverty occurrence lies in the widening gap in incomes of residents between regions, and between urban and rural areas. Different from the poverty caused by lack of basic living conditions seen thirty years ago, the current lack of basic public services and the shortage of public goods are important origins of the occurrence, accumulation and intergenerational transmission of poverty.

3. **The poverty issue remains prominent, and the poverty reduction drive faces new challenges**

As mentioned earlier, China has made remarkable achievements in poverty alleviation and development in the past two years, basically solving the survival and subsistence problems of the rural poor. According to the original poverty reduction standards, the rural poor population in China declined to 26.88 million at the end of 2010, achieving in advance the goal of halving the poor population among the UN Millennium Development Goals, thus making a significant contribution to global poverty reduction. However, we also must see that, as a developing country with a large population, a weak economic foundation and acute poverty issue, China faces a new situation and new problems in the work of poverty reduction.

Firstly, according to China's new poverty reduction standards, the rural poor population is huge. It is an international practice to raise poverty reduction standards in a timely manner in conformity with the reality of economic and social development.

Currently, eighty-eight developing countries have poverty alleviation standards. In the past two decades, thirty-five countries have raised their poverty reduction standards in a proper manner. In 1986, China set a poverty line of RMB206. In 2000, a two-track system was applied, setting a poverty line of RMB625 and a low-income line of RMB865. In 2008, the poverty line and low-income line were unified to be RMB1067. The line was further adjusted to RMB1274 in 2010. In the following year, China formulated a new rural poverty alleviation standard of RMB2300. As the new standards raised the poverty line, China's rural poor population will increase from 26.88 million to 128 million, accounting for 13.4% of the population with rural household register.

Secondly, the income level of the population in poor areas is low. Income indicator is a comprehensive indicator reflecting the poverty situation. From the practical point of view, the income of farmers in poverty-stricken areas has been less than half of the national average in the past decade. The per capita net income of farmers in key counties for poverty reduction was 59.40%, 53.0% and 55.3% of the national average in 2000, 2005 and 2010 respectively (see Table 4.5).

Third, the lack of infrastructure and public services in poor areas is still serious. At present, the infrastructure facilities in rural areas for water supply, transportation, communications and power supply lag far behind. The lack of basic public services such as medical care and education in rural areas is still serious (see Tables 4.6 and 4.7).

Table 4.5 Comparison between per capita net income of farmers in key counties for poverty reduction and the national average

Year	National average (yuan)	Key counties for poverty reduction (yuan)	Ratio of that of key counties for poverty reduction to national average (%)	Gap between that of key counties for poverty reduction and national average (yuan)
2000	2253	1338	59.4	−915
2001	2366	1276	53.9	−1090
2002	2476	1305	52.7	−1171
2003	2622	1406	53.6	−1216
2004	2936	1585	54.0	−1351
2005	3255	1726	53.0	−1529
2006	3587	1928	53.7	−1659
2007	4140	2278	55.0	−1862
2008	4761	2611	54.8	−2150
2009	5153	2842	55.2	−2311
2010	5919	3273	55.3	−2646

Source Rural household sampling survey and rural poverty monitoring survey by the National Bureau of Statistics

Table 4.6 Insufficiency of infrastructure facilities in key counties for poverty reduction and development in 2010 (unit: %)

Category	Scale
Proportion of rural households with difficult access to drinking water	8.9
Proportion of rural households in poor villages with difficult access to drinking water	9.9
Proportion of rural households with polluted drinking water sources	5.1
Proportion of rural households in poor villages with difficulty in obtaining fuels	34.4
Proportion of rural households without toilets	11.6
Proportion of rural households in poor villages without toilets	15.5
Proportion of natural villages without access to highways	11.9
Proportion of administrative villages without access to highways	0.5
Proportion of poor villages without access to highways	13.7
Proportion of natural villages without access to electric power	2.0
Proportion of administrative villages without access to electric power	1.2
Proportion of poor villages without access to electric power	2.9
Proportion of rural households in poor villages without access to electric power	2.8
Proportion of rural households in poor villages without heating equipment	43.6
Proportion of natural villages without access to telephone	7.1
Proportion of administrative villages without access to telephone	1.6
Proportion of poor villages without access to telephone	9.0
Proportion of natural villages without access to TV programs	4.4
Proportion of administrative villages without access to TV programs	1.7
Proportion of poor villages without access to TV programs	5.0

Fourthly, in the fourteen contiguous poverty-stricken areas, the poverty reduction task is difficult and arduous. According to the *Outline for Development-oriented Poverty Alleviation for China's Rural Areas (2011–2020)*, the government has designated fourteen contiguous poverty-stricken areas, encompassing 680 counties where the poverty reduction task is difficult and arduous. These areas are generally characterized by poor natural conditions, ecological fragility, weak financial and economic foundations, and low educational level of the population. Large numbers of households have become poor or slipped back into poverty due to the burden of high medical costs. Therefore, for these areas that have the highest incidence of poverty with the most difficult poverty alleviation tasks, the priority is to provide more policy support and funding from the country as a whole and all social sectors.

Table 4.7 Insufficiency of public services in key counties for poverty reduction and development in 2010 (unit: %)

Category	Scale
Dropout rate of children at the compulsory education phase	2.3
Proportion of population with illness who cannot seek medical treatment promptly	8.6
Proportion of rural households in poor villages who cannot seek medical treatment promptly	10.1
Proportion of labor force without skill training (male)	77.9
Proportion of labor force without skill training (female)	88.4
Illiteracy rate among laborers (male)	5.5
Illiteracy rate among laborers (female)	15.7
Proportion of poor villages without kindergarten/preschool	49.9
Proportion of poor villages without clinic among surveyed villages	19.8
Proportion of poor villages without qualified rural doctor/health worker	21.4
Proportion of poor villages without qualified midwife	24.7
Proportion of poor villages without professional technical training	55.6
Proportion of ethnic minority people in poor villages who cannot speak Chinese	26.8

Source Calculated according to the data of *Rural Poverty Monitoring 2010*, National Bureau of Statistics

4.3 Suggestions for Short- and Medium-Term Fiscal Policies

Achieving inclusive development is not only a long-term strategic goal, but also a major realistic and urgent task. It is of concern to all social sectors, and the central government has concentrated efforts to fulfill the remedial task. According to previous theoretical and practical analysis, the main idea for fiscal policy supporting inclusive development in the short and medium term is as follows: improving the policy and its coverage, increasing investment, clarifying the required direction and focus, grasping key points and resolving prominent contradictions, and effectively enhancing the pertinence, effectiveness and foresight of policies to gradually achieve the goal of inclusive development. Based on this, three policy suggestions have been put forward.

4.3.1 Fiscal Policy as a Means for Promoting Fair and Balanced Social Income Distribution

Narrowing the income distribution gap and building a fair and reasonable income distribution relationship are a major practical issue, requiring close attention from the government and all social sectors. It is of great significance in building a harmonious society and achieving truly inclusive development. The issue of income distribution concerns many aspects. The following are several suggestions from the perspective of fiscal and tax policies.

1. **Improving tax policy**

Tax policy plays a key regulatory role in adjusting income distribution. Reform focuses on four aspects: The first is to reform the system of individual income tax, an important tool in closing the income gap. Currently, China implements a classified income tax system. In order to achieve a fair tax obligation and narrow the income gap, the government has continuously raised the personal income tax threshold in recent years. However, this is still not enough to close the income gap, and eliminate an unfair tax obligation. Unlike practice in developed countries, China collects personal income tax on individual income, without taking into consideration relevant family financial burdens. Two individuals with the same income may face very different family burdens, but they must pay the same amount of tax under the current system. Therefore, China needs to implement a new tax system combining comprehensive consideration with classification by deducting expenditures on marriage, family support, education and elderly care from the pre-tax income. At the same time, efforts must be made to effectively strengthen tax collection management. Secondly, tax policies should be used to support employment and entrepreneurship, which are of paramount importance for ensuring and improving people's livelihood. Tax incentives should be given to special groups (e.g. college students, rural migrant workers and groups in special difficulties). The threshold for corporate income tax and business tax for small and micro enterprises can be further raised, while the tax rate can be reduced from 20% to 10%. At the same time, related fees can be adjusted or even canceled, and social security contributions can be postponed in a given period. The change from business tax to value added tax is a major reform, playing an important role in the reducing corporate tax burden, promoting the development of the tertiary industry, and expanding employment. It is recommended that, on the basis of expanding pilot projects in ten provinces and municipalities under the direct jurisdiction of the central government, the experience should be summarized to promote reform nationwide as soon as possible. Thirdly, property tax reform should be given greater priority. At present, the government measures operating in some cities to restrict purchases of houses are transitional, and need to be replaced by a property tax as soon as possible. It is necessary to fully understand the regulatory function of property tax on income and wealth distribution. Meanwhile, it has unique impact on the reasonable regression of house prices, prevention of bank risks, and long-term healthy development of the real estate sector and the overall economy. The recommended basic policy in regard to property tax is to include incremental houses and stock houses within the taxation scope, take appropriate per capita living space rather than the number of houses owned as the zero-bracket amount, and the evaluation value of house properties as the tax base. Real estate and property taxes should start at a low rate. Local governments of various localities should be given certain autonomy in tax collection under the premise of unified tax administration, and gradually develop property tax as the main tax paid to local municipal and county governments. Fourthly, tax policy for "third distribution" should be improved. It is a fact that, internationally, national income distribution is divided into primary distribution, redistribution, and "third distribution". As for this so-called third distribution, a certain amount of income from the wealthy class is collected through donations, charity and other means to support and help vulnerable groups. It is an important supplement to fiscal redistribution and an important way of social assistance. In this regard, we must earnestly learn from international experiences, actively encourage the development of philanthropy, enact a law for its promotion, establish and improve a mechanism of tax deduction for donations, and create a good social atmosphere for promotion of the third distribution.

2. **Improving fiscal spending policies**

The first aspect is to support social security reform, and increase the share of fiscal expenditures for social security. In the past ten years, China has made great efforts to reform the social security system, establishing a basic institutional framework. The long-term goal is to unify the urban and rural programs. However, there will certainly still be differences between the two in the near to medium term, but great efforts must be made to ensure the difference is narrowed continuously. With future economic development and the improvement of State financial capacity, the central and local governments should increase the social security expenditure share and subsidies in a timely and appropriate manner. At the same time, a social security fund budget management system should be established to ensure an effective safety valve for social stability. Both domestic and foreign experiences show that, due to the wide coverage, numerous items, involvement of the entire population, huge expenditure and rigid demand, we must pay close attention to the issue of fiscal sustainability, and prevent us from falling into the welfare trap and debt crisis facing Western countries. The second aspect is to make every effort to ensure equal access to education. As the starting point of social equity, this is an important way to narrow the development gap between different groups. It is necessary to improve the investment mechanism and the conditions for running schools, promote balanced regional development of education between urban and rural areas, and between different schools, and boost the allocation of public education resources to weak areas. Special attention should be paid to supporting equal acceptance of compulsory education for children of migrant workers in cities and towns, and gradually incorporate them into the scope of existing public schools in urban areas. The issue of discrimination in school enrollment existing for a long time has to be resolved. The third aspect is to support employment and entrepreneurship services. Poverty in urban families is correlative with the employment status of family members, and the difference in individual income is also closely related to the type of employment or the industry in which they are employed. Therefore, it is of vital importance to strengthen financial support for employment promotion and entrepreneurship. Work should be undertaken to stimulate entrepreneurial motivation for college graduates, rural migrant workers who have returned to their hometowns and other personnel, increase corporate training and entrepreneurial services, better implement and improve supportive policies to encourage enterprises, create an environment conducive to expansion of entrepreneurship, and raise its success rate. We must promote the transfer of surplus rural laborers for re-employment. The three-in-one working mechanism of vocational training, employment services and labor rights protection should be further improved, and prominent issues such as urban employment, settlement, children's schooling, and social security for rural migrant workers should be gradually resolved so as to promote the urbanization process actively and steadily.

3. **Adjusting the profit distribution pattern of state-owned enterprises and improving the state-owned capital management budget system**

Recent years have seen "the central government advances, while the private sector retreats" in China, and this has become an established fact. The excessive monopoly pattern of state-owned enterprises has tended to strengthen, and the relationship of distribution between the central government and enterprises is obviously unreasonable, becoming an important factor affecting fair income distribution. According to available data, the state-owned enterprises achieved a total profit of RMB1.3 trillion in 2009, and the figure rose 37.9% to nearly RMB2 trillion in 2010; the proportion of the profits turned over to the central government should be 5% to 10%, yet it was only 6% in 2009 and fell to 2.9% in 2010 on average. At present, the average proportion of listed companies' dividends to shareholders is 40% or so. In other countries, however, the dividends turned in by state-owned enterprises are generally 30–60% of their profits, and in some cases the figure is even as high as 80–90%. In addition, the dividends turned in by state-owned enterprises are mainly transferred within the enterprise system, without significantly benefiting the general public. In 2011, the total operating income of central state-owned capital amounted to RMB80.061 billion, and the expenditure reached RMB76.954 billion, of which RMB72.36 billion was returned to the enterprises in various guises, and only RMB4 billion was actually transferred to public finance for social security and other expenditures, accounting for 5.2% of the state-owned capital operating expenses. Therefore, the next step is to deepen the reform, adjust the profit distribution relationship between the central government and enterprises, and improve the state-owned capital operating budget system. The basic idea is to do a better job of collecting state-owned capital operating profits, promote reform of monopolistic industries and departments, and coordinate the state-owned capital operating budget expenditures. In combination with supporting reforms to eliminate the excessive monopoly of state-owned enterprises and through increasing the amount of state-owned capital operating profits turned into the central government, we can cut the earnings of corporate departments, reduce interference from state-owned enterprises with excessive monopoly profits and franchise incomes on market order, and directly increase government department revenue and concentrate more profits of state-owned capital to increase current transfers to the residents and improve people's livelihood. A concrete measure is to significantly strengthen the collection of state-owned capital operating budget revenue and make an overall plan for expenditures within the framework of the state-owned capital operating budget launched in 2007. Specific recommendations: first, the collection of state-owned capital operating revenue can first be strengthened in regard to the central state-owned capital operating budget. Adjustments should be made in regard to the current proportion of revenue collected in the process of promoting the in-depth reform of monopoly industries and departments, and the collection scope should be gradually expanded to include financial and state-owned enterprises affiliated to various ministries and commissions. In view of the characteristics of China's state-owned asset management model, "the State Council and the local people's governments shall, in accordance with laws and administrative regulations, perform respectively the contributor's functions for state-invested enterprises and enjoy the contributor's rights and interests on behalf of the central government". Therefore, local governments should be encouraged to establish a state-owned capital operating budget system and strengthen their management over income. Secondly, we must attach greater importance to the overall plan on state-owned capital operating budget expenditures in coordination with other budget funds in the public system. The scope of the existing "capital expenditure, expense expenditure and other expenditures" needs to be appropriately revised. State-owned capital operating income is, in essence, public revenue. For expenditures, we must adhere to the general principle that "assets are owned by the whole people and the benefits used by the entire people". The proceeds can be used not only for social security, but also for other public finance-oriented expenditures without obstacles through legal procedures where necessary. Moreover, this is also based on the premise of coordinating various budget expenditures and through a more powerful system of transfers from central finance, making it possible for local governments at all levels to share the profits created by central enterprises and solve a greater number of livelihood issues (Jia and Liu 2010).

4.3.2 Making Innovations on the Financial System and Distribution Mechanism to Promote Substantial Progress in Equal Access to Basic Public Services

Equality in basic public services is an important way to promote poverty reduction, and also a key means for achieving inclusive development. Recently, the government released the *Outline for Achieving Equality in Basic Public Services (2011–2020)*, which clarifies the scope, standards and policies involved. The next step is to implement the planning, carry out innovations in the financial system, and enhance the ability to ensure public financial security.

1. **Focusing on adjusting and optimizing the structure of fiscal expenditures**

According to the requirements of the market economy and China's current situation, the basic principle of the national fiscal expenditure structure in the future is to maintain expenditure in some areas while reducing it in others, and promote simultaneously incremental adjustment and stock adjustment. Only in this way can basic public services be supplied on a more reliable financial foundation. First, we must speed up administrative system reform, and effectively address the situation of institutional expansion, financial support for too many people, and cope with the heavy financial burden, so as to keep administrative expenses within a reasonable range. At the same time, we must continue to take measures to vigorously reduce spending on the "three public consumptions" (referring to spending official overseas visits, official vehicles, or official hospitality). Second, we must improve fiscal investment policies. Financial investment must be decisively withdrawn from the general competitive fields to narrow the current extensive scope. Third, we must concentrate financial resources and increase investment in the areas to improve people's livelihood, especially basic public services such as education, medical care, employment services, social security and ecological environment. Governments at all levels should prioritize budgets for basic public services, ensuring the growth rate of such financial investment matches resources and is adapted to the provision of basic public services, and promote an allocation based on the permanent residents in the region.

2. **Continuing to improve the transfer payment system**

It is necessary to further expand the scale of transfer payments, optimizing a structure that reduces financial differences between regions and achieves equality in basic public services, which are the goals designed for the financial transfer payment system, and let transfer payments play a better role in regulating local finances and promoting the equal access to public services. Firstly, the scale and proportion of balanced transfer payments should be enlarged. This is the most effective form of achieving equality, and yet, in 2009, the balanced transfer payment amount was only RMB391.8 billion, accounting for 16.5% of the total. Therefore, the amount and proportion should be gradually increased. It is recommended to increase the proportion by 10–15% age points during the 12th Five-Year Plan (2011–2015). In terms of capital allocation, we must continue to invest more in the central and western regions, helping them to strengthen ecological construction and environmental protection, increase our support for resource-exhausted cities and transfer payments to ethnic minority areas so as to accelerate their development. Secondly, we must improve the calculation method for balanced transfer payments with a view to promoting further equality in basic public services. To achieve this, the government should study and formulate standards for various types of services and gradually incorporate them into the scope of the system. While improving the calculation method for balanced transfer payments, we should give considerations to factors such as population size, population density, GDP per capita, the environment and ecosystem, altitude location, temperature range, and the resident population of ethnic minorities, as well as differences between administrative and public service costs, and, in accordance with actual conditions, adopt a standardized formulation method for allocation. Thirdly, the existing special transfer payments should be standardized. It is necessary to clean up and integrate existing special transfer payment projects, and strictly control the establishment of new ones. Those no longer meeting current actual needs and unsuitable for continued support through special transfer payments need to be canceled within a limited period; projects for similar purposes that can be merged should be so integrated; and those needing long-term relatively fixed subsidies should be included within the scope of general transfer payments. In addition, local government support for special transfer payments should be reduced. For expenditures that fall within the scope of the central authority, such as military and armed police expenditures, must be borne by the central government, with local support no longer required. In regard to matters involving a joint burden by the central and local governments that continue to need local support, due to the different fiscal systems of the various provinces involved, it is not advisable for the central government to uniformly specify the specific sharing proportions of provinces, cities and counties. The special funds involving local administrative power should gradually be canceled and included into general transfer payments. Fourth, we should explore the establishment of a horizontal transfer payment mechanism in the form of "counterpart support" with Chinese characteristics. This involves the mutual transfer of financial funds between local governments at the same level under the established fiscal system, in order to achieve mutual support between regions, reduce regional disparities and balance financial resources. Most countries in the world implement a single vertical transfer model, that is, through financial transfer payments from the central to local governments, and higher-level governments to lower-level ones. Only a small number of countries including Germany, Sweden and Belgium implement a mixed vertical and horizontal transfer model. As far as historical path dependence is concerned, although there is no standardized, formalized and legalized horizontal transfer payment system among local governments in China, "counterpart support" of this nature already exists. Developed areas in eastern China support underdeveloped areas in the central and western regions, which is conducive to accelerating the coordinated regional development and improving the overall economic development level of the country; this ultimately becomes a boon for the economic development of the eastern region. Therefore, it is advisable to pilot a horizontal transfer payment based on the current vertical transfer model. Fifth, it is necessary to improve the transfer payment management system and enhance the fairness and openness of transfer payments. We should actively utilize the formula and factor methods to scientifically and rationally allocate funds, minimize the arbitrary allocation of financial resources, and strengthen supervision over the use of the funds and performance evaluation. While disclosing the general transfer payment allocation method, the management method of funds for special transfer payment projects concerning people's livelihood should also be gradually made public so as to become more normalized and transparent, strengthening social supervision in the process.

3. **Speeding up the establishment of the basic financial security mechanism at the county level**

A basic financial security system at county level should be established for county finance to realize the "three guarantees" (covering issuance of wages, operations and people's livelihood) rather than the "two safeguards"(pay salaries, carry out normal operations, and safeguard the wellbeing of their residents) approach that excludes the latter factor. This is an important part of the upcoming financial system reform below provincial level, and also an institutional innovation that fundamentally resolves the grassroots financial difficulties of counties and townships, and promotes equality in public goods provision at the provincial level. In recent years, the central government has taken a range of measures to alleviate the financial difficulties of counties and townships with initial good results. The next step is to speed up the establishment of a basic financial security mechanism at county level. Specific suggestions are as follows: First, the reform spirit and policy orientation should be clarified. A basic financial security system at county level should be established step-by-step with clear goals, local governments taking the main responsibility and the central government providing subsidies and rewards. The goal is to ensure that the basic financial capacity of a county government is strong enough to realize the "three guarantees", promote equality in county-level financial resources and coordinated social and economic development at this level. To adapt to the basic financial security mechanism requirements at county level, local governments should take the main financial responsibility. The central government can give special subsidies to underdeveloped areas and appropriate rewards to the counties that do a good job in realizing the "three guarantees". After having gained experience through pilot work, we can then gradually implement the system nationwide. Second, the goal of realizing a basic financial security mechanism at county level should be realized through institutional innovation. The principle of "setting no ceiling limit and giving no minimum guarantee" should be changed into that of "setting no ceiling limit and giving the minimum guarantee" so as to further consolidate and expand the achievements in alleviating the financial difficulties of counties and townships. Through the current reform of provincial management over counties, a provincial government allocates funds to corresponding county governments, which also turns in revenue to the former; however, no fundamental breakthrough has been achieved in the reform in terms of administrative power, revenue and expenditure scope, and transfer payments. For this reason, in order to build a basic financial security system at county level, further reforms should be undertaken in increasing the bonus funds, strengthening provincial regulatory capacity, and improving relevant security measures. According to the goals of the plan, the financial burden method should be rationally determined. After the introduction of the new mechanism to ensure people's livelihood, policy coverage and extension have become relatively large. Although the central government has continued to increase the subsidies and rewards, the guiding role is still insufficient, and there should be a large expansion in this regard. Based on this, according to the current financial capacity and people's livelihood in central and western China, a financial burden approach that is more conducive to the realization of the goal, promotes the overall progress, and has a significant effect can then be determined. To scientifically determine the scope, standards and financial needs of the county-level "three safeguards", we must enlarge the coverage rate and raise the guarantee level. In terms of the latter, higher-level governments should provide policy funds to guide counties with strong financial capacity to bring into full play their endogenous power. For those with poor financial resources, higher-level governments should offer encouragement through greater adjustments.

4. **Actively promoting innovation of the basic public service supply mechanism**

To transform government functions and improve administrative efficiency, innovation of the public service supply mechanism is a necessity and also an important way to improve the efficiency of public service supply, promote equality in basic public services, and ensure more equitable earnings for the poor. Firstly, the public service supply strategy should be improved to ensure low-income and poor groups can benefit equally and fully from basic public service projects. Attention should be paid to reducing and possibly eliminating the various barriers blocking access to basic public services for the poor. For example, in the process of promoting equality in basic public health services, when designing various types of services, full attention should be paid to their timeliness and availability for the poor and low-income groups, enabling them to benefit more widely and in a fair way. Secondly, a diversified supply mechanism of basic public services should be set up to vigorously expand social poverty alleviation. On the principle of government-led development of public welfare undertakings, we should explore diversified supply, give full play to the active role of social organizations in their provision, establish a market mechanism and improve the efficiency and quality of public services. In some aspects, including basic education, health care and employment training, we should undertake bold reform of traditional budget allocation and the mode of direct organization and provision by the government, and explore and innovate in regard to an effective supply mechanism. For example,, the traditional practice of allocating funds for education and healthcare can be replaced by issuance of "education/health vouchers"; restrictions on the qualifications for making investments in basic public services should be relaxed; and the system of investment in basic public services of government should be reformed through tendering, contract rental, franchising, and government participation in share issuance. The direct supply function of the government should be delegated to market players as much as possible. The government's main responsibility then can be shifted to financing and supervision. Third, it is necessary to establish and improve the mechanism of basic public service demand and interest expression. An appropriate public goods demand and interest expression mechanism should be established and improved for poverty-stricken areas to fully meet their needs, preferences and priorities, and so on.; this need can be turned into a reference and a goal for policy and decision making through a set of procedures. Establishment and improvement of such a mechanism is of great significance for maintaining the relative balance between supply and demand of local public goods, reducing waste of public resources, lightening the burden on farmers, safeguarding the reasonable rights and interests of rural poor, improving the relations between cadres and the masses, safeguarding the reasonable rights and interests of rural poor people, and maintaining social stability. We should gradually establish a government administrative commitment system, a hearing system, and an information inquiry and consultation system to ensure that basic public service supply fully reflects social demand.

4.3.3 *Strengthening Financial Support and Vigorously Promoting Poverty Reduction and Development in Concentrated Contiguous Poor Areas*

In view of higher poverty reduction standards, a larger poor population and the fact that China's economic development has entered a new stage, the approach to poverty reduction will naturally undergo major changes, that is to vigorously promote poverty reduction and development in concentrated and contiguous poor areas. In view of greater fiscal responsibility, the following countermeasures need to be undertaken.

1. **Establishing and improving a diversified governmental and social investment mechanism for poverty alleviation**

Poverty alleviation is a public welfare undertaking, so the government finance department plays an important guiding role in solving problems. However, poverty reduction and development in poor areas involve industrial development, public service provision, and steps to promote income growth for residents in poor areas. The single channel of finance alone is far from sufficient. It is necessary to establish a diversified governmental and social investment mechanism for poverty alleviation. First, we should ensure a reasonable increase in fiscal investment in poverty alleviation. The increase of fiscal poverty alleviation funds must be compatible with government functions, national financial growth, poverty incidence, and poverty alleviation and development needs. Both central and local governments have the responsibility to increase poverty alleviation investment and a due proportion of poverty alleviation funds in overall budget expenditure. Second, the central government should allocate more transfer payments to poor areas. The local per capita financial capacity should be taken as the core factor for achieving equality in transfer payments, and the share of special transfer payments for poor areas must be increased. More provincial-level transfer payments should also be weighted toward the latter. Third, credit funds for poverty alleviation should be gradually increased. It is necessary to study and formulate credit poverty alleviation strategies and policies, guide banks to increase investment in poverty alleviation, and reduce the interest burden on loans for poverty-stricken areas through improvements in the fiscal discount policies. Fourth, enterprises of various economic sectors, in particular private enterprises and foreign capital, should be encouraged to invest and develop in poverty-stricken areas. On the basis of implementing preferential fiscal and taxation policies, we must pay attention to creating a good investment environment and convenient conditions.

2. **National public policy should be favorable to poor areas**

Rural anti-poverty actions must be integrated into the overall plan for national economic and social development, and relevant national policies must be appropriately favorable for the poor areas and the poor. Firstly, it is advisable to implement differentiated industrial development policies. It is advisable to formulate the Catalogue of Industries Encouraged in Develop in Poverty-stricken Areas and the

Catalogue of Priority Industries for Foreign Investment, giving preferential policies in terms of project approval, investment and land use, and so on. Secondly, we should increase State investment in poor areas. More special fund investment of relevant State departments should be made in contiguous poor areas, and the investment subsidy standards or the proportion of capital injection in construction projects such as highways, railways, civil aviation, water conservancy and forestry should be increased. Thirdly, it is important to formulate preferential land policies. In regard to the incremental construction land quota, priority should be given to meeting the requirements of relocation and house construction in the contiguous poor areas, and support should also be given to the exploration of new ways to improve the quality of supplementary arable land on the premise of supplementing the same area of arable land to maintain the balance between occupation and supplement of arable land. Fourthly, we should reasonably determine the energy conservation and emission reduction indicators and the main pollutants emissions in the contiguous poor areas. The degree of industrialization in poverty-stricken areas is generally low, and their economic development is subject to environmental constraints. Considerations should be given to regional differences when setting relevant environmental constraint indicators. At the same time, the central government must give greater support for the elimination of backward production capacity and the closure of inefficient small businesses in poor areas. Fifthly, supporting funds should be provided by local governments in the contiguous poverty-stricken areas to compensate for the cancellation of central government subsidies. The local supporting policy has been implemented for many years aimed at mobilizing the investment enthusiasm of local governments. However, poor areas with limited financial resources often cannot support such programs, and there are even cases of false or insufficient provision of supporting funds. Therefore, for various public welfare construction projects arranged by the central government in the contiguous poor areas, it is necessary to cancel the supporting funds provided by governments at and below county level. Sixthly, preferential tax policies should be implemented. It is necessary to support the development of poor areas through tax reductions and exemption, investment tax credits, reduced taxable income, and weighted deduction. At the same time, the reform of resource tax should be promoted. In accordance with the unified deployment, taxes for the products appropriate to be levied on an ad valorem basis rather than on specific basis, and the tax rates of some ferrous, non-ferrous metal ores and other non-metal ores should be raised appropriately.

3. **Clarifying the focus and direction of national capital investment and policy support**

In the new era, how to change the backward state of the contiguous poverty-stricken areas as soon as possible? It is of significance to put out focus on the support and make clear where the funds will go. The first step is to break through the constraints of infrastructure bottlenecks. Due to the contiguous impoverished areas are mostly located in mountainous and remote areas with poor infrastructure facilities, financial resources should be concentrated on solving the urgent problems of poor areas in regard to such items as safe drinking water, provision of roads, power supply, communications and encouragement of small water conservancy facilities. Meanwhile, renovation of farmers' dilapidated houses in poor areas must be eligible for State subsidies. The "one project, one discussion" policy for rural infrastructure facilities should be tilted in favor of poor areas. In areas with poor living conditions deemed unsuitable for human habitation, the poor residents should be relocated gradually. The second step is to expand the leading industries for poverty alleviation. We should continue to support advantageous traditional characteristic industries. Many large grain-producing counties are very poor. The government must increase grain purchase prices, provide greater support for agricultural production, increase the transfer payment share of key grain-producing counties, and link the grain yield and transfer volume with the rewards and subsidies of major grain-producing counties to actively support grain production in poor areas. National policies and poverty alleviation funds should provide necessary support to some poverty-stricken areas that focus on cultivating leading poverty alleviation industries such as potato cultivation, economic trees and fruits, grassland husbandry, cotton planting and other leading industries. In addition, we should also actively support the development of emerging industries such as tourism, environmental protection and energy saving industries, the new energy industry, or strategic emerging industries in poor areas, which is a strategic move to optimize the industrial structure and develop the economy in poor areas. The third step is to enhance their self-development capabilities. The key is to strengthen poverty alleviation through education. We must establish a stable growth mechanism for public funding of primary and secondary schools in poor areas to ensure their average per capita education expenditure reaches the national average by the end of the 12th Five-Year Plan (in 2015) so as to consolidate and improve the compulsory education level in poor areas. It is necessary to vigorously develop free vocational education so that students from poor areas who have not yet entered high schools or universities can immediately receive vocational education to learn professional skills.

4. **Building a model of integrated urban and rural development and a public policy system that benefit all the poor in the long run**

In the long run, China must establish a policy system and development model that can benefit vulnerable groups and enable them to share the fruits of integrated urban and rural development, and avoid the widening gap, estrangement and tension between rich and poor during the urbanization process in developing countries. First, the government should vigorously support the development of labor-intensive industries and ensure the stable employment of a large number of rural laborers in cities and towns. Training programs for migrant workers have proven successful in China and elsewhere. For example, in the Indian state of Andhra Pradesh, after three months of training for vulnerable young workers, they can be offered employment options in urban or suburban areas; in Bangladesh, similar short-term training for poor rural families has also proven successful, providing skills training and food assistance for them to work in cities or urban suburbs. Second, a unified and equal market of productive factors for both urban and rural areas should be built. A reform of "non-elite" household registration system should be carried out to enable most urban employees to reach the threshold of household registration. It is advisable to provide real and complete property rights for rural land, and realize the same right and same price for urban and rural construction land. Fair "compensation" must be given to landless farmers. Third, an integrated public service policy system for urban and rural areas rather than a fragmented system should be established to cover both urban and rural residents and build a national livelihood safety net covering vulnerable urban and rural groups. Many rural migrant workers covered by social insurance programs choose to withdraw from the program after a time because they feel they cannot enjoy the benefits brought to them by the insurance after they move. In addition, when they withdraw from the insurance, they can only get back the share of these funds they pay themselves; however, the insurance money paid by their employers for them remains in the places of their work. In order to solve the problems of rural migrant workers, the existing plan itself needs to be extended, and new independent projects should be launched to meet the special needs of rural migrant workers. Taking into account the different levels of economic development of various provinces and the constraints of the current fiscal transfer payment policy, the central government should give certain support and encourage provincial governments to implement a provincial system of coordinated urban and rural public services first, and then promote this nationwide when conditions are ripe. Fourth, it is necessary to establish a financial transfer payment system combining "personal jurisdiction" and "territorial jurisdiction" and giving special care to the poor. Public services such as education, medical care, endowment insurance and poverty alleviation should be provided under a mechanism of subsidies based on "personal jurisdiction" instead of "territorial jurisdiction". Fifth, we should give full consideration to the accessibility of rural left-behind people to basic public services as well as the greater demand for urban public service funds caused by urbanization and the basic needs of vulnerable rural left-behind people for public services when allocating financial funds so as to benefit left-at-home groups via due fiscal transfer payments and avoid further marginalizing such vulnerable groups (UNDP Task Force 2010).

References

Asian Development Bank. (2010). *Poverty, inequality and inclusive growth in Asia*. China: China Financial and Economic Publishing House.

Feng Z., & Feng, H. (2011). The scientific meaning of "inclusive growth" and its world historical significance. *Journal of Jishou University*, No. 1.

Kang, J., & Wei, L. (2010). Thoughts and suggestions on financial and tax policies to increase the "two proportions" in national income distribution and contain the widening income gap. *Research Report*, Research Institute for Fiscal Science of Ministry of Finance, No. 93.

Su, M. (2010). Financial policy positioning and suggestions for implementation of the western development strategy. *Research Report*, Research Institute for Fiscal Science of Ministry of Finance, No. 95.

Su, M., et al. (2011a). Research on China's fiscal system reform, *Review of Economic Research*, No. 50.

Su, M., Liu, J., et al. (2011b). *Equalization of basic public services and poverty reduction in the context of changing economic model*. China: China Agricultural Press.

The Yearbook of China's Poverty Alleviation and Development 2011. China: China Financial and Economic Publishing House.

United Nations Development Programme and International Poverty Reduction Center in China. (2010). *Towards a more inclusive poverty reduction strategy: Key challenges and recommendations* (exposure draft).

World Bank. (1997). *The state in a changing world*. China: China Financial and Economic Publishing House.

World Bank. (2008). *Strategies for sustainable growth and inclusive development*. China: China Finance Press.

Chapter 5
Population and Employment Policies as Instruments for Facilitating Inclusive Development

Fang Cai and Meiyan Wang

Since the reform and opening up program was launched some forty years ago, along with economic system reform and rapid economic growth, China has managed to build up a social policy system meeting the needs of the socialist market economy. These policies have the salient feature of sustainable development and showing great concern for people's livelihood. Since the start of the present century, more contents have been added to support the concept of inclusiveness. A policy oriented to coordinated development of population, resources and environmental protection, and an employment policy targeting full employment and sharing achievements of economic development constitute an important part of this inclusive approach. This paper introduces the salient features and effects of formulating and implementing the population and employment policies in China, while identifying urgent challenges in both areas, and puts forward some suggestions for future policy adjustment.

5.1 Population Policy: Content, Effects and Evolution

5.1.1 Shaping of Population Policy and the People-Oriented Starting Point

Since the 1970s, the central government advocated a family planning policy featuring an approach of "late, spacing and fewer" (i.e. late marriage, adequate birth spacing and fewer births) until formal adoption of what became known as the "one-child

F. Cai · M. Wang (✉)
Institute of Population and Labor Economics, Chinese Academy of Social Sciences, Beijing, China
e-mail: wangmy@cass.org.cn

C. Zuo et al. (eds.), *Inclusive Development and Poverty Reduction*,
International Research on Poverty Reduction,
https://doi.org/10.1007/978-981-15-8446-6_5

policy" in the 1980s. This family planning policy achieved great success over subsequent decades. The population policy, whether in terms of formulation or implementation, has always aimed at improving the lives of the people both materially and culturally. The *Open Letter on Issues of Population Growth from the CPC Central Committee to the Whole Party and Communist Youth League Members* (Open Letter for short hereafter) released on September 25, 1980 was actually the official announcement of the family-planning policy. Adopting the approach of a heart-to-heart talk, the Open Letter explained that the family planning policy "is a major measure of vital importance to the progress and prospects for modernization construction and to the health and well-being of future generations, and is in line with the long-term and immediate interests of people of the country".

In 1991, the CPC Central Committee and the State Council issued the *Decision on Strengthening Efforts on Family Planning and Strictly Controlling Population Growth*. The Decision reiterated the established policies and demanded maintenance the stability and continuity of these policies,[1] while further emphasizing tight control of population growth. Afterwards, family planning regulations were formulated by various provinces, autonomous regions and municipalities under the direct jurisdiction of the central government in line with local conditions. With the approval of the standing committees of the local People's Congresses, these regulations were implemented as a local law. Work to improve the family planning policy nationwide came to an end in the early 1990s.

The formulation of the family planning policy was closely related to Deng Xiaoping's plan to develop China's economy in "three steps". From the late 1970s to the late 1980s, Deng worked hard to undertake wide-ranging research, consult with others and study the feasibility of goals such as "quadrupling GNP", "creating a well-to-do life" and "USD800 in annual per capita income" before the end of the 20th Century (Yang 2011). Based on in-depth research, evaluation and the practical development of the national economy, Deng explained the "three-step" strategy for economic development during a meeting with foreign guests on the eve of the 13th National Congress of the CPC in 1987: first, to double the 1981 GNP and ensure the provision of basic material needs by 1990s; second, to double the 1991 GNP by the end of 20th century and bring people's living standards to a level of "reasonable prosperity"; and third, to quadruple that new GNP to the level of moderately developed countries by the mid-21st century, and bring the Chinese people an affluent life and achieve basic modernization.

In 2002, the 16th CPC National Congress made a major decision concerning China's reform and opening up and modernization drive: On the basis of the original "three-stage" strategic plan for modernization, in the first fifty years of the 21st century, China would spend the first two decades (2001–2020) "concentrating on its strength to build a higher-level better-off society benefitting more than one billion people" as " an inevitable connecting link for attainting the third-step strategic objectives for our modernization drive". Maintaining coordination among population

[1] *Decision of the CPC Central Committee and the State Council on Strengthening Family Planning and Strictly Controlling Population Growth*, ZF [1991] No. 9, May 12, 1991.

control, husbanding of resources and environmental protection became an important guarantee for building a well-off society in an all-round way.

Thus it can be seen that the strict one-child policy evolved from the early government call for voluntary birth control to the promulgation of the Open Letter in 1980, showing China's population policy basically served the implementation of China's national strategic plan, conducive to speeding up economic development and improving people's living standards as soon as possible.

5.1.2 Changes in Execution Mode and Incentive Mechanism of the Population Policy

China's population policy, being people-oriented as the starting point, was implemented by adopting an incentive mechanism and various measures featuring advancing with the times. In the early days of adoption of the family planning policy, the policy goal was some distance from people's fertility intentions. It was implemented mainly through administrative means with the result that many people were dissatisfied, making it difficult to implement.

With the gradual decline in the birth rate, however, the birth control policy was then implemented in new ways. Former administrative measures made way for incentive guidance, and implementation paid more attention to service and care, and through redoubled publicity efforts. Meanwhile, an interest-oriented policy system was introduced in a preliminary way; the policy system mainly comprised of a family planning reward system, focused on "having less [children] and getting rich more quickly", and a special support system. High-quality family planning services and birth care activities were carried out in a general way. New customs in regard to marriage and childbirth emerged, Care for Girls Action and new family planning concepts were further promoted in rural areas.

China's current birth control policy has taken shape as a result of prolonged practice. It embodies unified requirements of the law, and is introduced by fully taking into consideration the actual situation in localities. With the change in population situation and socio-economic development, the policy has been repeatedly adjusted. A concrete birth control policy has been undertaken based on local population and family planning rules and regulation. Very often, China's family planning program has often been referred to as the "one-child policy", which, in fact, is incorrect. Owing to unbalanced economic and social development, family planning policy is implemented differently among regions, between urban and rural areas, and between the Han ethnic group and ethnic minorities. Overall, the policy is implemented loosely in the rural areas compared to cities and towns, in western China compared to eastern and central China, and in areas where ethnic minorities live in compact communities compared to areas inhibited by the Han ethnic group. According to current practice, the overall fertility rate conforming with the birth control policy is about 1.47, and about 60% of the population implement the one-child policy.

In recent years, while maintaining the stability of the current fertility policy, local fertility policies have been slightly adjusted across the country. For example, local governments of various provinces, autonomous regions and municipalities under the direct jurisdiction of the central government allow couples who themselves are only children to have two children. In Tianjin and Shanghai (municipalities under the direct jurisdiction of the central government) and the five provinces of Liaoning, Jilin, Jiangsu, Anhui and Fujian, when one of the rural couples is an only child, they can have two children; in Jilin, Hainan, Gansu, Hunan, Zhejiang, Shanxi, Hubei, Guangdong and Jiangxi Provinces, Shanghai (municipality under the direct jurisdiction of the central government), and Inner Mongolia and Xinjiang (two autonomous regions), the regulations have either been abolished or relaxed on birth interval; and Hebei, Liaoning, Jilin and Guangdong Provinces and Xinjiang Uygur Autonomous Region practice relaxed restrictions on remarried couples.

5.1.3 Unprecedented Demographic Shift: Fertility Decline

The implementation of the population policy and economic and social development have resulted a sharp fall in the fertility rate. From 1970 to 1980, China's total fertility rate dropped sharply. However, in the early 1980s, the total fertility rate was still above replacement level. The adoption of strict family planning policy in 1980, and, then even more importantly, thanks to the rapid economic and social development under the reform and opening up program, birth rate eventually dropped below the replacement level of 2.1 in the early 1990s (Fig. 5.1).

After that, China's total fertility rate continued to decline and remained below 1.5 for years (Gu and Li 2010). According to the U.N. statistics, China's total fertility rate stood at 1.4 in 2006, compared to a global average of 2.6. From 2005 to 2010, the total fertility rate in developed regions averaged 1.6, while that in underdeveloped regions (the least developed countries excluded) was 2.5. China has ranked among those countries with the lowest fertility rate in the world for some time (UN 2010).

5.1.4 Positive Effects: Contribution of Demographic Dividend to Economic Growth

China's rapid economic growth has benefited significantly from the demographic dividend throughout the development period of the dual economy since the reform and opening up. This conforms with the trend anticipated by economic theory with Chinese characteristics, and can be confirmed by statistics. The contribution of the

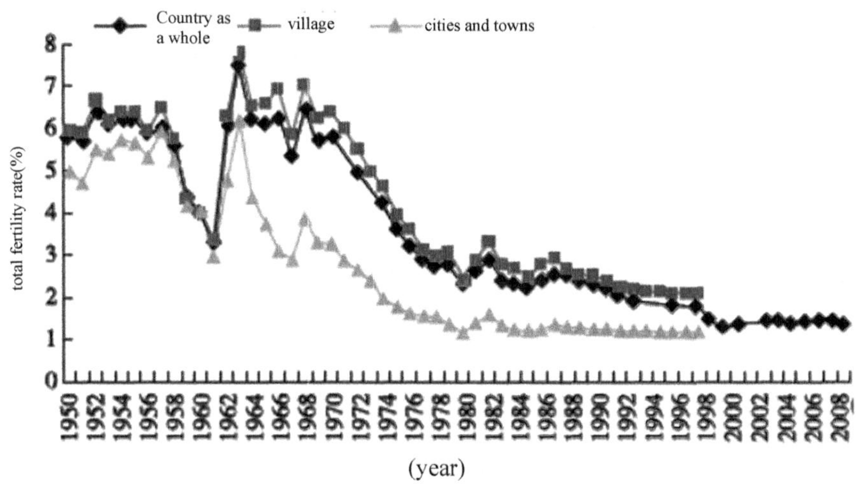

Fig. 5.1 Declining Trend of Fertility Rate in Urban and Rural Areas of China. *Source* Calculated according to database of China Population Information and Research Center before 1998, and data of sample surveys of population thereafter

demographic dividend to economic growth falls in the following four aspects to power economic growth.[2]

First, the continuous decline of the population dependency ratio has provided a strong foundation for capital formation in the period of rapid economic growth, and helped the national economy to maintain a high savings rate. This factor is reflected in the contribution rate of capital.

Second, sustained growth of working-age population guarantees sufficient labor supply. And with the improvement of the educational level of its workers, China has been able to maintain a significant low-cost advantage of its labor force with equivalent quality amid the process of economic globalization. The effect of those factors on economic growth lies in the contribution to the increase of variables—labor input and human capital accumulation—in the production function.

Third, the transfer of a massive force of rural surplus labor during the reform has shaped resource relocation efficiency by creating a flow of labor from low-productivity sectors to high productivity ones, becoming the main source of total factor productivity.

Fourth, if the population dependency ratio is taken as an explicit proxy variable of demographic dividend, its contribution to economic growth can be taken as demographic dividend in the pure sense.

Through the method of production functions, a research into China's economic growth since the early 1980s observed the relative contribution of various factors to

[2]A report from the RAND Corporation points out that the demographic dividend is achieved by increasing the supply of labor, savings and the investment and return of human capital. See Bloom et al. (2002).

economic growth during the ongoing reform and opening up program. These factors took fixed capital formation, the employment rate of the whole society, years of formal education of the work force, dependency ratio and residuals as variables, which respectively stood for the contribution of capital investment, labor input, human capital, demographic dividend and total factor productivity to the GDP growth rate. The results showed that, in regard to GDP growth between 1982 and 2009, the contribution rates of capital investment, labor input, human capital, human capital, population dependency ratio and total factor productivity were 71.0%, 7.5%, 4.5%, 7.4% and 9.6% respectively (Cai and Wen 2012).

5.2 Pro-active Labor Policies and Their Effects

The acquirement of a demographic dividend is premised on full labor employment. The reform and opening up program has brought China the greatest labor flow and largest employment scale of the world. The active employment policy that promotes urban and rural employment and the reform aimed at promoting the development of the labor market play a very important role amid the process.

5.2.1 The Establishment and Improvement of Active Labor Market Policies

Through long-term efforts, and having paid a heavy price overall, China has gradually formed a framework of active employment policies. Before the reform of employment system in the late 1990s, the urban labor market mechanism played the main role in allocating new workers. The state-owned and collective enterprises accommodated the vast majority of such a work force. At the time, economic growth was considered to be synonymous with employment growth, and not the focus of macroeconomic policy alone. In the expression of monetary and fiscal policies at that time, there was no independent place for employment.[3]

Affected by the Asian financial crisis in the late 1990s and the slowdown of domestic economic growth, state-owned enterprises got into unprecedented difficulties leading to unprecedented layoffs and unemployment in the nation. In response to this grim situation, and in order to guarantee the basic livelihood of the people, the central government started to adopt active employment policies and rolled out a set of policies geared to promote employment and re-employment. At the same time, employment was also taken as an objective of macro-economic policy, its importance being upgraded ever since. Active employment policies focused on using training and services to adjust the labor supply, using macroeconomic regulation to

[3]Please refer to (Cai 2009) for a summary of this aspect.

promote economic growth and expand employment, regulate labor market demand, and broaden the range of employment and job channels to the greatest possible extent.

On September 12, 2002, Jiang Zemin, then General Secretary of CPC Central Committee, delivered a speech entitled *Employment Has a Vital Bearing on the People's Livelihood* at the national work conference on re-employment. In the report, Jiang talked about the extreme importance of the work on employment and re-employment which he said should be fully recognized. How well the employment issue was handled should be used as an important indicator measuring the level of good governance by the CPC and the government, and should, therefore, be the top priority of both. At the 16th National Congress of CPC Central Committee held in the same year, the main report proposed to take employment promotion as the long-term strategy and policy for the Party and government, with strong efforts to boost economic growth, promote employment, stabilize commodities prices and maintain the balance of international payments as the main macroeconomic objectives. From this we see that expanding employment has been placed in a more prominent position in economic and social development, and promoting employment has been taken as a priority development strategy.

To reverse the adverse impact of the 2008 global financial crisis on China's economic growth and social development, the government proposed to adopt more active employment policies; efforts were made to "ensure employment" to meet the goal of "sustaining economic growth, ensuring people's wellbeing and maintaining stability". The 12th Five-Year Plan reaffirmed the importance of actively promoting job creation as a strong policy foundation for full employment, which not only made clear the priority position given to employment in overall government policy-making, but also helped to focus on key areas for expanding employment and targeted key groups for government employment assistance.

5.2.2 Labor Market Development and Employment Expansion

China's rapid economic growth has always been accompanied by rapid expanding employment (Cai 2010). However, many researchers thought employment growth was not keeping pace with economic growth mainly because they were confused by incomplete and inconsistent parts of the available employment statistics. Firstly, laborers transferring out of rural areas weren't included in urban employment statistics. By 2011, the number of rural laborers who left their hometowns for more than six months or more had reached 158.6 million (Organization of Rural Socio-Economic Survey, National Bureau of Statistics 2012). Secondly, since the late 1990s, non-regular employment mainly consisting of new workers and re-employment of laid-off workers wasn't incorporated into the sectoral and region-based employment statistics, hence this part of employment being missed in any analysis using non-aggregated data. And this part of the labor force amounted to over ninety million in

2009, accounting for 28.9% of the employment of urban residents.[4] Moreover, rural laborers working in nonfarm industries in their hometown were also often neglected by researchers. This segment of the job market didn't increase noticeably, but its stock cannot be ignored, as it represented a stable payroll close to 100 million people.

In order to obtain a more complete picture of employment and labor supply, we try to break up a single statistical source to reveal the actual level of urban employment, and take it as agent information of nonfarm labor demand. As the absolute number of laborers working in the agricultural sector is decreasing year by year, and nonfarm employment in rural areas is relatively stable, we could omit agriculture and non-agriculture employment in rural areas, only basing our work on surveying the employment growth of rural migrant workers and urban residents.

According to calculations based on available data, among the 310 million urban employees in 2009, about 38.96 million were rural migrant workers, accounting for 12.52%, far less than the actual number. If we assumed that migrant workers were not included in the urban labor survey in 2000, and their proportion rose at certain pace in following annual surveys, i.e. it rose to 12.52% in 2009, and continued to grow at the same pace, then we may figure out the percentage of migrant workers in urban employment statistics each year, and the number of urban employees apart from migrant workers.

In addition, we also knew there were 145 million rural workers who had been away their hometown for six months or above by the end of 2009, and 95.6% of them had moved to urban areas. Supposing the distribution of rural migrant workers remained stable over the first decade of the new century, we can work out the total scale of rural migrant workers on the basis of the annual Monitoring Survey Report on Migrant Workers by the National Bureau of Statistics. Now, let's take a look at the annual stock of these two employment factors, and compare them with the national stock of the working-age population (See Table 5.1).

As we can see, from 2001 to 2011, urban employment increased significantly faster than the growth of the working-age population, indicating China's economic growth is not jobless growth. On the contrary, the expansion of urban employment accompanying urbanization cannot be ignored. As a manifestation of the effectiveness of active employment policies, surplus agricultural labor, urban unemployment and redundancy have been greatly reduced.

5.2.3 Labor Mobility: Effect on Poverty Reduction and Income Growth

The poverty level in rural areas has been reduced as a whole as a result of rural migrant workers able to earn more than if they had remained to undertake farm work; even if this has not led to a narrowing of the income gap between urban and rural areas, it does have the effect of restraining expansion of the gap. As the household contract

[4]Calculated according to the data of *China Statistical Yearbook (2010)*.

Table 5.1 Changes in Labor Supply and Demand Unit: 10,000 people, %

Index Year	Employment of urban residents (1)	Migrant workers in cities and towns (2)	Working age population (3)	Demand-supply ratio (1) + (2)/(3)	Demand-supply elasticity Δ[(1) + (2)]/Δ(3)
2001	23,607	8,029	88,536	35.7	–
2002	24,091	10,009	90,070	37.9	4.5
2003	24,569	10,889	91,399	38.8	2.7
2004	25,003	11,303	92,893	39.1	1.5
2005	25,430	12,025	94,352	39.7	2.0
2006	25,947	12,631	95,234	40.5	3.2
2007	26,492	13,094	96,009	41.2	3.2
2008	26,848	13,423	96,757	41.6	2.2
2009	27,224	13,894	97,419	42.2	3.1
2010	27,669	14,627	98,059	43.1	4.4
2011	27,955	15,165	98,622	43.7	3.4

Source Calculated according to the data from *China Statistical Yearbook* (calendar year), *China Yearbook of Rural Household Survey* (calendar year), *China Population Statistics Yearbook* (calendar year) and Du and Hu (2011)

responsibility system based on equal distribution of land ensures that labor mobility is a voluntary choice to pursue higher income and a better life, the expansion of the labor mobility scale is enough to significantly increase the income of farming families even if the wage rate remains unchanged. The effect of labor mobility on the income of rural families can be observed from following three aspects.

The first is the effect of labor mobility on poverty reduction. Except for rural families with insufficient labor resources or poor employability, many poverty-stricken families are poor because of inadequate employment. Moreover, previous studies have shown non-farm employment opportunities in rural areas tend to be obtained by those with skills, or coming from an influential family, while most of poverty-stricken families have no access at all. Hence, going outside as a migrant worker means an opportunity to gain a higher income. A study shows that poor rural households may improve household net income per capita by 8.5% to 13.1% in this way (Du et al. 2005). Undoubtedly, poverty-stricken families short of labor and human capital in general are often unable to overcome the obstacles in transfer, and cannot fully benefit from the dominant labor flow.

The second aspect is the contribution of wage income to the increase in farmer household prosperity. According to work of the National Bureau of Statistics, net income of farmer households consists of four kinds—wage income, household business operation net income, property income and transferred income. The increased availability of out-of-town job opportunities significantly helps improve farmers' wage income and enhance its proportion in household income, so as to become the main source. According to official statistics, the share of wage income of farmer households rose from 20.2% in 1990 to 41.1% in 2010, while the contribution rate of wage income in the net income increment of farmers stood at 48.3% in 2010.[5]

The third aspect is the wage income of migrant workers missed by household surveys carried out within the statistical system. Since these are carried out independently in urban and rural areas, income of rural families whose members have left their hometown to work in cities and towns is largely missed. Moreover, because they are no longer taken as residents of rural areas, their income is not included in rural household surveys. According to *China Statistical Yearbook*, people who live in other places for more than six months, but bring their main income back home are still taken as permanent residents of their original households in view of the economic ties they maintain with their families. However, those living outside their hometown all year round (not including those who return for family visits, medical care, and so on.) and have stable jobs and living abodes are no longer considered permanent residents and their income cannot be reflected in household income of their original domicile.

Therefore, incomes of migrant workers have, to a large extent, been underestimated. Many scholars have noticed the improving trend of income distribution, and have sought relevant evidence from an imperfect statistical system. Seeking to overcome the defects of existing systems covering urban and rural household income statistics, Gao Wenshu and his research team selected Zhejiang, a developed province in east China, and Shaanxi, a less developed western province for a fresh detailed study. They surveyed households with an account kept by the relevant statistical bureaus, and sample households, seeking to reevaluate the income of rural migrant workers missed both by urban and rural surveys. They found loopholes in the official household statistical survey that led to over-estimating the disposable income of urban residents by 13.6% and underestimating the net income of rural residents by 13.3%; the conclusion is that the income gap between urban and rural areas has been overestimated by 31.2% (Wenshu et al. 2011).

5.2.4 Construction of the Labor Market System and Labor Rights and Interests

During the late 1990s, a large number of enterprise workers were laid off. To cope with the situation, the Chinese government adopted active employment policies, including a more extensive social security system, macroeconomic regulation and control based on the principle of expanding employment, active support for re-employment, including training and creation of public welfare jobs. In response to the adverse impact from global financial crisis that hit the world in 2008–2009, the Chinese government's new policy was reinforced by adoption of a series of new measures described as "more active employment policies".

[5]Calculated according to the data of *China Yearbook of Rural Household Survey.*

With the reduction of agricultural surplus labor, labor shortages appeared and became persistent in various related industries and sectors. Under the situation, the government adopted new measures to benefit "rural areas, agriculture and farmers", and enhanced the comparative advantages of farming. These were all conducive to the improvement of the bargaining chips available to laborers, especially migrant workers, in negotiations for an improved employment relationship. As a result, wages for various industries were increased in an all-round way, the gap between the wages of skilled and unskilled workers narrowed, and working conditions improved faster than before.

Since 2004, the central and local governments undertook more active and effective efforts to improve the policy environment for migrant rural workers to gain better access to urban employment opportunities, residential conditions and equal public services by way of legislation, law enforcement, adjustment policies, etc. Although institutional changes and policy adjustments needed further improvement, many observers felt growing rural labor mobility under the reform and opening up program marked a turning point as the policy environment for such labor mobility entered a golden period in 2004 (Cai 2010).

At the same time, labor market system construction was promoted by accelerating the introduction of a series of laws and regulations such as the labor contract law and reinforcing law enforcement efforts concerning labor relations. At the request of the central government, local governments pushed to raise the minimum wage. And a normal, regular wage increase mechanism for ordinary workers gradually formed.

5.3 New Policies Needed to Keep Up with Change in Development Stage

China's rapid growth beginning in the 1980s has been characterized as a typical dual economic development. Alongside the demographic shift there is the massive transfer of agricultural surplus laborers and the expansion of urban employment. With the demographic transformation and economic development of China reaching a new stage, this mode of economic development is bound to be concluded through a series of transitions.

5.3.1 The Arrival of the Two 'Turning Points'

In 2004, the eastern coastal areas suffered from a shortage in the supply of migrant workers, and this problem subsequently became a national problem. In 2011, China's manufacturing industry suffered from unprecedented difficulties in recruiting rural labor as a whole. While the growth rate of the labor supply slows down, economic growth continues to maintain strong demand for labor, and urban employment continues to grow rapidly. The change in labor supply and demand relationship has brought to an end the situation in which China's resource-based industries as a whole enjoyed limitless supply of workers; the marginal productivity of labor in agriculture is no longer as low as the theoretical hypothesis, and wages are no longer determined by the level of survival, but are more sensitively affected by supply-demand relationship.

Having hovered around a given level, the wages of migrant workers started to rise in 2004 in a remarkable way, registering an increase of 12.7% between 2004 and 2011.[6] So far as the manufacturing and construction industries are concerned, wages in these sectors where more unskilled workers are employed grew at an annual real rate of 10.5% and 9.8%, respectively, between 2003 and 2008.[7] Judging from the change in wages of workers employed from rural areas, in the period from 2003 to 2009, payments to rural migrant workers increased at an average annual rate of 15.3% in grain production, 11.7% in cotton production and 19.4% in large-scale pig farming.[8]

By the definition used in development economics, this shortage of labor and constant rise of wages for ordinary workers means China has reached its Lewis turning-point. Although there are different views on this judgment and the applicability of the Lewis model in China, the great challenges to the country's economic growth brought about by such changes deserve high attention.

As a result of the long-term decline in fertility levels, the age structure has changed accordingly. So far, the working age group between 15 and 64 has continued to increase; however, the growth rate has been decreasing year by year and is expected to stop growing around 2013. At the same time, the dependency ratio (i.e., the dependency-to-working-age population) decreased to the lowest point before rapidly rising again (Fig. 5.2). Just as the researchers often use the dependency ratio as a dominant proxy indicator of the demographic dividend, the reversal of the dependency ratio change trend marks a turning point as the demographic dividend fades away.

From this, we can see the year 2004 could be taken as the landmark year when China reached the Lewis turning point, while 2013 is when the demographic dividend fades away. Obviously, the length of time between these two turning points is directly related to characteristics of the demographic shift. It is the premature aspect of China's demographic shift (or "getting old before getting rich") that is most worrying.

According to research, Japan reached the Lewis turning point around 1960 (Minami 1968). If the increase of dependency ratio is taken as the turning point in the disappearance of the demographic dividend, this turning point came in 1990, which means there was a 30-year gap between them. The Republic of Korea got to the Lewis turning point in 1972 (Bai 1982), and its demographic dividend faded around 2013, the same time as China did, but with a 40-year interval.

[6]Calculated according to the data of *China Yearbook of Rural Household Survey.*

[7]Calculated according to the data of *China Labor Statistics Yearbook.*

[8]Calculated according to the data of the *Compilation of National Agricultural Product Cost and Income.*

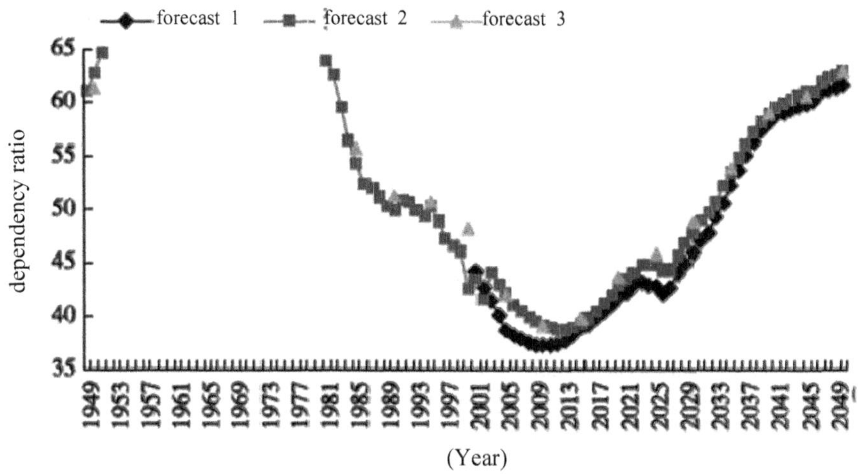

Fig. 5.2 The End of Falling Dependency Ratio Means Demographic Dividend Is Gone. *Source* Forecasts 1, 2 and 3 by Hu Ying, Wang Guangzhou and the United Nations, respectively

When taking 2004 as China's Lewis turning point and 2013 as the moment when the demographic dividend disappeared, the two are only nine years apart. This characteristic of China not only explains why labor shortages have become very strong as soon as they arise, but also warns of the urgency of the challenges in transforming growth patterns and adjusting policies.

5.3.2 New Trends and New Tasks in the Labor Market

The arrival of Lewis turning point means that the dual structure of the labor market is fading, and a series of characteristics marking a mature labor market are looming. In countries with a mature market economy, employment pressure is mainly manifested in three types of unemployment, namely, cyclical unemployment caused by macroeconomic fluctuations, structural unemployment by mismatch between workers' skills and employer demand, and frictional unemployment by people hunting jobs for too long. The structural and frictional modes are the norm of unemployment, both relatively stable and stubborn, so it is also referred to collectively as natural unemployment. China will face growing incidence of these three types of unemployment in the future.

Under the conditions that the market allocates resources and guides economic activities, the cyclical fluctuations of the macro-economy are inevitable, and the corresponding cyclical unemployment phenomenon is also unavoidable. In China's current stage of development, rural migrant workers in urban areas often have to bear a greater cyclical impact of unemployment because of their rural hukou [residential registration card] and unstable jobs. For example, the impact of the 2008 international financial crisis on China's real economy and employment resulted in the early return of tens of millions of migrant workers to their hometowns before the advent of the 2009 Spring Festival that fell on January 26 that year. That was one case of cyclical unemployment.

With the acceleration of industrial structure adjustment, some traditional jobs will inevitably disappear as new employment opportunities are created. Workers who need to be transferred but fail to adapt their skills to the requirements of their new positions will face the risk of structural unemployment. As China's labor market development is still at a low level and the human resources allocation mechanism is far from perfect, workers cannot undergo job transfer without friction in the industrial structure changes. As a result, frictional unemployment will often occur. The groups of newly developed workers, including all kinds of graduates who are better educated than many others, need a process of matching their human capital with the demand of labor market. As for those living in cities and towns lacking new skills, there will be more friction in dovetailing demand of labor market. Hence, these two groups of workers are most vulnerable to these two types of unemployment.

5.3.3 Challenges to the Demographic Structure

Thanks to a tight family planning policy and continuous economic development, China has succeeded in controlling the size of its population. However, structural problems continue to emerge. The challenges are mainly reflected in the following aspects:

First, the gender ratio of the new-born population remains highly unsatisfactory in terms of an imbalance between male and female births, with the latter set at 100. Since the fourth census in 1990, the ratio has significantly exceeded the normal range. In 2009 it was still as high as 119.5 boys to 100 girls. Gender discrimination in the labor market and an inadequate social security system are the main causes of the gender imbalance of the population.

Second, there is a rapid increase in population aging. Such an aging trend is the inevitable result of economic and social development, and the irreversible trend of population development. An "aging society" with the elderly population accounting for a large proportion of the total population becomes the norm as people live longer and families become smaller. However, China is experiencing a situation of "getting old before getting the rich", posing serious challenges to the country's endowment ability, pension security system and socio-economic development. Therefore, it is necessary to redouble efforts to speed up improvements in the basic old-age insurance system covering all urban and rural residents, developing a strong social consensus on helping and respecting the aged and improving national capacity to provide for them, and carry out strategies featuring a "positive, healthy, guaranteed and harmonious" approach in tackling the aging population.

Third, the quality of population does not meet the requirements of economic and social development. The overall education level is still relatively low, with an illiteracy rate of 7.8% among people aged fifteen and older in 2008, and the span of formal education averaging 8.5 years. The overall incidence of birth defects across the country continues to rise, with apparent congenital malformations at birth and gradually emerging defects afterwards accounting for 4% to 6% of the total birth population and about eight-hundred thousand children born with birth defects each year. There are 82.96 million persons with various disabilities in the country. The situation of reproductive health is simply not optimistic.

5.4 Improve Policies to Promote Comprehensive Population Development

Formation of the population policy, characterized by family planning, was closely related to the original planned economy and then the national conditions of the dual economic structure, a necessity with the passage of time. In the current language, the initial intention was to maximize the release of the demographic dividend in the short term. China is now in a new stage of economic development and demographic transition, and the trend of population change is undergoing important changes. New population conditions are taking shape.

To better plan the future in order to do a good job in all aspects of population development and gradually improve the policy, we should still start from the principle of maintaining the sustainability of economic growth and seeking improvements of people's living standards. To balance population development so as to become a truly positive factor for sustainable development calls for improvement in terms of quality, structure and quantity and other aspects; in other words, efforts should be made to achieve substantial improvement in the quality of the population itself, achieve a rational age structure and gender ratio, and ensure the sustainability in terms of quantity. In following sections, we will make a number of policy recommendations from three important perspectives: education development, efforts to cope with the aging population, and fertility policies.

5.4.1 Improving Overall Human Capital

After the disappearance of the first demographic dividend, not only the traditional elements driving economic growth need to be reorganized, but also higher demands are raised for more long-term effective economic sources that are not prone to produce diminishing returns. In particular, a significant increase in the national overall human capital level is required to create a second demographic dividend while avoiding the middle-income trap.

First of all, compulsory education remains a stage for students to lay a good foundation for lifelong learning, the key part of the education process in creating an equal starting line for children from families at different income levels and from both urban or rural areas. It is the government's bounden duty to fully invest in this process. Pre-school education has been recognized as creating a higher social rate of return. That the government pays for it conforms with the law of education and the principle of benefiting the whole society. Hence, pre-school education should be gradually included into the scope of compulsory education.

In recent years, with increasing job opportunities, there is the strong demand for low-skilled workers. Some children, especially those from poor rural families, have tended to drop out of junior high school, and this is a serious issue to be addressed. The government should significantly reduce the proportion of household expenditure in compulsory education, so as to consolidate and enhance the completion rate. By integrating pre-school education into the compulsory educational system, children from the rural areas and poverty-stricken families will not lose out at this crucial early stage. In greatly helping to improve their completion rate in primary and secondary schools, it also increases equal opportunities to continue with further study.

Second, we should greatly improve the level of high school enrollment and promote the popularization of higher education. The enrollment rates of high schools and schools of higher learning promote each other and interact in terms of both cause and effect. An expanded high school attainment rate means a larger number of people willing and able to go on to colleges and universities; more opportunities for enrolment in colleges and universities will inspire more youngsters to attend and complete the full range of high school education. At present, the proportion of expenditure in the government budget is low in regard to the high school stage, and the burden of family expenditure is excessively heavy. This, plus the high opportunity cost and the low success rate of being admitted to a university, makes high school education a bottleneck for the future development of education (Cai and Wang 2012). Therefore, in order to promote rapid popularization of higher education, the government should promote free education at this stage as soon as possible. Comparatively speaking, higher education should give full play to the enthusiasm of the whole society and families to invest in it.

Finally, vocational education should be vigorously developed under the guidance of the labor market. China needs a great number of skilled workers, whose cultivation depends on secondary and higher vocational education. The proportion of school-age students in Europe and the United States, who receive vocational education, is usually above 60%, and the figure is even as high as 70% to 80% in countries such as Germany and Switzerland, all significantly higher than the Chinese level. China should start from the requirements of medium- and long-term development in the quality of workers, and increase vocational education and vocational training. Moreover, efforts should be made to establish a channel between vocational education in high schools and professional higher education and regular higher education, speed up reform of the education system, teaching mode and teaching content, so that students can have more choices to achieve all-round development.

5.4.2 Actively Responding to the Aging of Population

China's aging population has entered a period of rapid acceleration. By the end of the 12th Five-Year Plan [in 2015], China will still be in the middle-income stage of development, while the number of people aged sixty and above will exceed two-hundred million, or about 15% of the total population. China's sustainable development needs to meet the serious challenge posed by population aging characterized by "getting old before getting rich".

First, efforts should be made to improve the social pension security system by expanding coverage of both urban and rural residents as well as the transient population, and to improve the level of security and overall planning, and form a strong source of provision for welfare of the aged. Full pension coverage for urban and rural residents should be achieved as soon as possible, and social services for the aged should be vigorously developed, so as to effectively protect and gradually improve living standards of the elderly, especially those without family and ones with disabilities. An aging population exerts influence on innumerable households and raises concerns about social harmony and sustainable development. Under the premise of the government ensuring the provision of relevant basic public services, work should be undertaken to comprehensively enhance the joint efforts combining society, family, community and industries related to the elderly, to vigorously promote the construction of a service system for the aged supported by financial security and service assurance, and focus on consolidating home-based care for the aged, expanding community support, enhancing institutional service capacity, and promoting the development of a strong service industry for the aged.

Second, efforts should be undertaken to tap the new consumption demand provided by the aging population and turn it into a driving force for economic development. The elderly comprises a special consumer group whose cultural needs included keep-fit activities and recreation, as well as wide-ranging provision of material needs for the home-based and the institutional care of the aged. The central government should give them support and encouragement through funding, taxation breaks, finance and business administration, so that such demand generated by the inevitable aging trend will promote the formation of some new service industries and become a new driving force for economic development.

And last, measures should be adopted to properly develop human resources of the aged, create suitable jobs for them, and explore a flexible retirement system. At present, for every one year of age increase among Chinese people aged between twenty-four and sixty-four, the number of average years of education decreases by 10.2%. The older the age group, the more notable the progressive decrease of the educational level. For those between the ages of 44 and 64, their average schooling years decrease by 16.1% for each year of age increase (Wang and and Niu 2009). It can be seen that the conditions for raising the retirement age are not yet mature, and it is urgent to create mature conditions through the development of education and training, so that the labor participation rate of the elderly in the future can be raised to alleviate the pressure from insufficient resources of social provision for the aged, and extend the period of the demographic dividend.

5.4.3 Gradually Improving Fertility Policies

China's population policy needs to be readjusted in line with the times under the premise of a people-oriented concept. Although demographic transitional changes are ultimately driven by economic and social development, the trend of population aging is, inevitably, difficult to reverse. However, under the premise of adhering to the basic national policy of family planning, there is still much that can be done.

First, there is still room for China to promote future population balance through policy adjustment. According to various surveys, the average number of children expected to be produced by a couple is about 1.7 based on the current fertility intentions of Chinese families. The policy fertility rate, that is to say, the number of children policy allows, stands at 1.47, comparable to the actual total fertility rate. It can be seen that there are still some differences between the level of policy fertility and fertility intentions.

Second, according to policy expectations, the birth control policy has successfully completed its historic mission. According to an announcement by the CPC Central Committee in 1980: "Thirty years from now, the problem of population growth, which is particularly intense even today, can be alleviated and a different population policy can be adopted." Today, the given condition of adopting "different population policies" (i.e. the total fertility rate falling to a lower level) is much more mature than ever expected. Therefore, a sufficient policy basis is available for policy adjustment.

And thirdly, the practice of local policy adjustment provides a road map for reform. At present, majority of provinces have allowed families where both spouses are from a single-child family to have a second child (commonly known as the "double-single" policy). This move hasn't produced significant fertility changes. Following this path, once the policy evolves to the point that, when couples where one spouse is an only child can have a second child (i.e. a "one-single" policy), the coverage of the policy adjustment will be extended to a wider population range, which may have a long-term effect on birth equilibrium.

5.4.4 Creating Systemic Conditions for Gender Equality

The discrimination against women in the labor market, and the deep-rooted concept of "raising children for one's old age" prevailing when the social security system is far from adequate have combined to become a major cause of gender imbalance. This problem should be tackled by addressing both symptoms and root causes in a comprehensive way, such as walling up gender discrimination in employment through the promotion of gender equality, eliminating gender bias in fertility by improving the social pension system so as to effectively curb the rising trend of sex ratio at birth.

Law enforcement efforts through use of the employment promotion law should be strengthened to eliminate discrimination against women in the labor market. This kind of discrimination often takes two forms: wage discrimination and employment discrimination. The former means the employer pays female employees lower wages than their male counterparts holding the same post with the same productivity level. The latter form means the employer deliberately assigns female employees to the lower-paid posts while reserving higher-paid ones for males, even though there is no significant difference in productivity. Thus, efforts should be made to strengthen the implementation of labor laws to supervise and create equal opportunities, and eliminate wage differentials between men and women in the same posts. In addition, the labor market should be actively cultivated to reduce system barriers on access to employment.

5.5 The Need for More Inclusive Employment Policies

With the arrival of the Lewis turning point and the end of the original demographic dividend, Chinese employment issues have gradually transformed from the contradiction led by total quantity to a structural one. This change adds new meanings to active employment policies, creating a new mission to enhance inclusiveness. Now, we offer proposals in the following aspects, including the focus of employment policies, the establishment of integrated labor market and labor market system.

5.5.1 Shifting Focus from Total Quantity to Structure

To deal with the increasingly prominent cyclical, frictional and structural unemployment, we should first establish the principle of giving priority to employment in the formulation of macroeconomic policies, set up an appropriate policy direction and intensity on the basis of employment status, so as to reduce the risk of cyclical and natural unemployment. In the 12th Five-Year Plan (2011–2015), the government seeks to expand the job market to assume a more prominent position in economic and social developmental strategy.

In order to ensure priority is given to employment, the overall macro-control requirements should consider not only the GDP growth target, but also directly the goal of employment growth and the control objective of the surveyed unemployment rate that could reflect the level of cyclical unemployment. Focusing on employment goals and the control objectives of unemployment, a reasonable rate of economic development should be determined, and maximizing employment should be taken as an important consideration in determining the direction, measures and efforts of macro-control policy, in order to reduce the impact of economic fluctuations on employment. Meanwhile, expanding employment needs to be established as a common reference to better meet the need to reduce unemployment by strengthening coordination and cooperation between finance, banking, tax and other macroeconomic policies.

Structural and frictional employment difficulties shouldn't be taken lightly in a tight labor market. The groups of new workers including various types of graduates and disadvantaged groups in urban areas without the necessary new skills to meet the demands of industrial changes are the most vulnerable to such types of unemployment. This is the most suitable area for government to promote employment. It also demands improved functions in the labor market and higher government public service capacity, which means the government is required to offer more targeted training including that for employment, entrepreneurship, job transfer and on-the-job training, to standardize and improve human resources market functions, in order to lower natural unemployment by improving abilities of the workers and market allocation efficiency.

5.5.2 Promoting the Integration of Urban and Rural Employment

A labor market institution that allows free movement of labor and effectively protects the legal right to employment provides the necessary institutional guarantee by which a middle-income country may transit to a high-income one. At present, there are still a variety of institutional obstacles in China's labor market impeding labor mobility, including the division of urban and rural areas, regional segmentation and separating the household register and identity, which prevents equality in job opportunities and the rational and efficient allocation of human resources. Efforts should be made to get rid of these institutional barriers as soon as possible, help urban and rural workers to gain equal access to employment opportunities, and further improve labor market institutions. Therefore, we should continue to adhere to the principles of making overall urban and rural development plans, further improve relevant policies, deepen system reform, and promote a stable transfer employment trend among rural labor.

Policies aimed at achieving system reform should, in the process of formulation and implementation, focus on related areas where migrant workers are apt to be included into the social security system, as well as gain equal access to public services. At present, in accordance with the statistics of permanent resident population, China's urbanization rate has reached 51%, but the proportion of the population with nonfarm registered permanent residence is only 34%, which means a significant proportion of nonfarm migrant workers still cannot enjoy equality in their access to basic urban public services. The central government has explicitly pushed reform of household registration system and relaxed the requirements for household registration in small and medium-sized cities, enabling farmers with stable employment and residence in urban areas to become urban residents in an orderly and legal manner.

Starting from the principle of incentive-compatibility, one of the available means to advance urbanization is to provide a more stable security and protection for employment of migrant workers by the establishment of an efficient labor market system. On this basis, the construction of the system can be gradually promoted to a wider range of public services, to help achieve urbanization in the true sense and the synchronization of urbanization with the non-farming population, so that we may pass smoothly through the Lewis turning point and the dual economic structure transition.

5.5.3 Labor Market Institutions Construction and Social Protection

The arrival of the Lewis turning point is a clear sign of dramatic changes in labor relations. Under the new situation of supply and demand of labor, workers are demanding improvement of wages, benefits and working conditions along with gaining increasing awareness of their rights, while enterprises do not show a matching willingness of displaying poor adaptation, which is bound to lead to local conflicts between the employers and the employees. Facing such "growing pains", adopting an evasive attitude, or promoting populist policies that cannot sustain a long-term commitment, won't solve the problem. It is the system construction on which we may successfully transit the middle-income stage.

Due to concern about system of collective consulta6tion on wages, it became the weak point of system building of the labor market. In fact, comparing with the situation in Europe and America, it would be more controllable and easier to achieve positive results by building a collective consultation system on wages and working conditions on the basis of the current institutional framework in China. A labor relation pattern with Chinese characteristics might be explored when the union represents the interests of workers, the entrepreneurs association acts on behalf of the interests of employers, and the government functions as the force for guidance, coordination and consultation in the system.

Social protection covers a broader range than the labor market institution in terms of functions. Moreover, it can integrate the labor market, social security and other social welfare systems in line with the concept of building a harmonious society, and shape a public service system adapting to the socialist market economy with Chinese characteristics, so as to realize and ensure the "people-oriented" principle. After the arrival of the Lewis turning point, with labor shortages gradually formed a constraint on economic development, the Chinese government should strengthen social protection of labor and promote the rights of all residents.

References

Bai, M.-K. (1982). The turning point in the korean economy. *Developing Economies*, (2), 117–140.

Bloom, D. E., Canning, D., & Sevilla, J. (2002). *The demographic dividend: A new perspective on the economic consequences of population change*. CA, RAND: Santa Monica.

Cai, F. (2009). On the priority of employment in social and economic development policies. In the *Selected Works of Cai Fang*. China Publishing Group, Zhonghua Book Company.

Cai, F. (2010). The formation and evolution of china's migrant labor policy. In Z. Xiaobo, S. Fan & A. de Haan (eds.) *Narratives of Chinese Economic Reforms: How Does China Cross the River*? New Jersey: World Scientific Publishing Co. Pte Ltd.

Cai, F., & Wang, M. (2012). On the status quo of China's human capital—how to explore new sources of growth after the disappearance of the demographic dividends. *Frontiers*, 6.

Cai, F., & Wen, Z. (2012). When demographic dividend disappears: Growth sustainability of China. In M. Aoki & J. Wu (eds.) *The Chinese Economy: A New Transition*, Basingstoke: Palgrave Macmillan, Forthcoming.

Du, Y., & Hu, Y. (2011). *Forecast of Working-age Population from City-country Dimension*, unpublished background report.

Du, Y., Park, A., & Wang, S. (2005), "Migration and Rural Poverty in China", *Journal of Comparative Economics*, Vol.33, No.4, pp.688-709.

Gu, B., & Li, J. (2010). *The Debate on China's Population Policy in the 21st Century*. Social Sciences Academic Press.

Hu, Y., Cai, F., & Du, Y. (2010). Demographic change during 12th five-year plan period and forecast of future demographic Trend. In F. Cai (ed.), *Reports on China's Population and Labor—Labor Market Challenges in the Post-crisis Era*. Social Sciences Academic Press.

Minami, R. (1968). The turning point in the japanese economy. *The Quarterly Journal of Economics, 82*(3), 380–402.

The Organization of Rural Socio-Economic Survey, National Bureau of Statistics of China. (2012). *China Yearbook of Rural Household Survey*. China Statistics Press.

United Nations. (2010). *World Fertility Pattern, 2009*, http://www.un.org/esa/population/publications/worldfertility2009/worldfertility2009.htm.

Wang, M. (2011). Urban Employment, non-farming employment and urbanization. In F. Cai (ed.), *Reports on China's Population and Labor (No. 12)– Challenges during the 12th Five-Year Plan Period: Population, Employment, and Income Distribution*. Social Sciences Academic Press.

Wang, G., &Niu, J. (2019). Status, issues and trend projection of china's population education. In F. Cai (ed.), *Reports on China's Population and Labor—Reforming the Education System to Promote Human Capital*. Social Sciences Academic Press.

Wenshu, G., Wen, Z, & Jie, C. (2011). The impact of rural labor flow on statistics of income gap between urban and rural residents. In C. Fang (ed.) the *Reports on China's Population and Labor (No. 12)—Challenges during the 12th Five-Year Plan Period: Population, Employment, and Income Distribution*. Social Sciences Academic Press.

Yang, F. (2011). On the Shaping of the 'Three-Step' Development Strategy of Deng Xiaoping, *Guangming Daily*, August 3, 2011.

Chapter 6
Promoting Inclusive Development by Supporting Technological Innovations in Rural and Agricultural Development

Jingdun Jia

6.1 New Opportunities for Inclusive Development

6.1.1 World Economy and Social Development Face Heavy Task of Accelerating Transformation After the International Financial Crisis of 2008

The international financial crisis of 2008 triggered in the U.S. had a broad and far-reaching impact on the world economy and the international community in general. At that time, overheated development of the real estate industry and the financial sector made the expected return on investment far greater than the actual industrial return; this broke the basic economic principle requiring balance between income and expenditure, and caused a serious rupture in the industrial capital chain, seriously damaging normal development of the financial industry and the real estate industry. The trans-regional, cross-industry and cross-border penetration of modern industries, especially the financial sector, had a huge derivative, destructive impact over a wide area. The financial crisis seriously affected the real economy, causing serious social problems such as rising unemployment. Existing imbalances in trade and economic development, shortage of resources and energy, food security, poverty, population aging and unemployment, and sovereign debt problems, further magnified the adverse impact, which still exists, and all countries are continuing efforts to restore stable economic growth and improve people's livelihood.

Counter-measures taken worldwide to restore stable global economic growth include such initiatives as adjustment of the financial industry and its enhanced supervision, providing greater self-examination of existing development modes, economic

J. Jia (✉)
China Rural Technology Development Center, Ministry of Science and Technology, Beijing, China
e-mail: gaoj@ssap.cn

C. Zuo et al. (eds.), *Inclusive Development and Poverty Reduction*, International Research on Poverty Reduction,
https://doi.org/10.1007/978-981-15-8446-6_6

restructuring, and leading to exploration of new development modes, as well as technical innovations, and development of strategic emerging industries, particularly those related to the real economy. All of these efforts have been made to achieve higher-level sustainable development. During the 12th Five-Year Plan for National Economic and Social Development [2011–2015], China focused on transforming its economic development modes and adjusting the economic structure, which is of great significance in addressing the financial crisis, solving various problems and achieving long-term development. In fact, the financial crisis also created new opportunities and a fresh driving force for transformational development of the international economy. What is different from the past is that the need for concerted and coordinated action by the international community so that it can cope with any future international financial crisis in the era of further globalization.

6.1.2 New Challenges from Global Climate Change

Tackling global climate change is a common challenge for the international community. The history of addressing climate change is actually a course of scientifically coordinating the relationship between development and protecting the ecological environment, and coordinating national responsibilities and obligations at different stages of development. However, the expected results have not been achieved in addressing climate change. In 1992, delegations of 183 countries, and representatives of seventy international organizations including the United Nations and its affiliates, attended the U.N. Conference on Environment and Development held in Rio de Janeiro, at which several important documents were adopted, including *Agenda 21, the United Nations Framework Convention on Climate Change, the Statement of Principles on Forests*, and *the Rio Declaration on Environment and Development*. It marks a great step by the international community, including both developed and developing countries, in forming a consensus on resolutely addressing global climate change through practical actions. Twenty years on, the U.N. held the "Rio+20 Summit" (United Nations Conference on Sustainable Development), mainly discussing the role of the green economy in promoting sustainable development and eradicating poverty, as well as an institutional framework of sustainable development. This reflects the international community realizes the urgent need to achieve sustainable development.

The strategic measures taken to effectively cope with global climate change involve changing the traditional economic development modes. In the second half of the 18th century, an industrial revolution occurred involving the establishment of a scientific and technological system based on fossil energy, fundamentally transforming the way the global economy and industries developed. Fossil energy and mechanical equipment became the basic props of the global economic growth mode. This mode of production, featuring huge productivity, brought about tremendous wealth to humanity, and fundamentally changed the relationship between the economic industry and the ecological environment, but caused serious ecological damage, environmental pollution and huge consumption of resources and energy. Heavy consumption of fossil energy gives rise to huge greenhouse gas emissions. This increase is a key factor in global warming. Over the years, climate anomalies and extreme climate disasters have occurred with increasing frequency, seen as an inevitable outcome of global climate change. The economic development mode with a history of over two hundred years must be changed radically in order to minimize greenhouse gas emissions, and achieve green development and harmony between economic growth and a fragile ecological environment.

In 1987, the World Commission on Environment and Development defined sustainable development as one meeting the needs of contemporary people while not endangering the wellbeing of future generations. This definition in the report entitled *Our Common Future* was widely recognized. In the past two decades since the United Nations Conference on Environment and Development in 1992, all countries have put sustainable development in a high position, but the results have fallen short of expectations.

(1) The global population has increased by 27% to more than seven billion, which is mainly contributed by West Asia, Africa, and South America. The relationship between humanity and nature becomes increasingly tense.
(2) Global temperatures have risen by 4 °C on average, with the maximum rise in the past 10 years occurred after 1998.
(3) Carbon dioxide emissions have increased to thirty billion tons from 22 billion tons in 1992.
(4) Forests and tropical rain forest coverage has decreased by three hundred million hectares.
(5) The number of megalopolises each with a population of more than ten million has risen to twenty-one from the ten existing in 1992.
(6) Consumption of plastics as one of the largest pollutants has increased to 265 million tons from 149 million tons in 1992.
(7) The situation of hunger and poverty remains severe. Since 1970, more than a billion people have been certified as suffering from long-term hunger, 98% of whom live in developing countries, particularly those in the Asia-Pacific region and Africa. According to the Multidimensional Poverty Index released by the United Nations in 2010, there are 1.7 billion poor people in the world today.

These figures demonstrate the problems of population, poverty, resources and environment have become more serious, and global sustainable development has not been properly achieved; what's more, the situation continues to grow in seriousness. Addressing a series of identified major international issues is directly related to global stability and sustainable development. All countries must take more effective actions to transform economic growth modes, minimize resource consumption, ecological environment damage and pollutant emission, and explore new development modes to achieve global economic and social development in harmony with ecological environment.

6.1.3 New Changes in Social Development

Income imbalance is a global problem, which has been further intensified since the 2008 international financial crisis. It is estimated that the world's poorest people (40% of the global population) hold only 5% of the world's total wealth, while the richest group (20% of global population) own 75%. Such an imbalance of wealth distribution has aggravated social contradictions. Underemployment and high unemployment rates, in particular, have caused intense social conflicts or unrest in some countries. For example, strikes, social unrest and social turmoil are often seen in several EU member states affected by the European debt crisis, such as Greece, Spain and France, which is mainly attributed to poor economic development and severe unemployment. China also faces the problem of income imbalance, which is reflected particularly in the huge income gap between urban and rural residents. In 2011, per capita net income of Chinese farmers was RMB6,977, while the per capita disposable income of urban residents was RMB21,810.

Population aging results in the occurrence of new problems. It has become increasingly severe in developed countries. Japan has been an aging society since the 1970s, the population aged sixty-five or above accounting for 23% of the total. Europe is a similar case. Having a far-reaching impact on modern society, population aging increases social expenditures and the burden on the central government, families and the social economy, while reducing the labor supply. In EU countries, population aging and high social welfare spending, to a certain extent, have further increased the governmental financial burden and created additional structural difficulties for economic recovery and growth.

The cost of living constantly rises in modern society amid a continuous improvement in living standards. People are gradually bidding farewell to the traditionally frugal life. With the development and continuous progress of science and technology including that of industry, people are spending more time on education and training to acquire more knowledge, leading to increased personal expenditure and also higher social cost.

Population mobility is a prominent issue. In various countries, uneven economic development and different living standards give rise to a new social problem—cross-regional population mobility involving social and economic development. In 2011, there were 250 million rural workers in China, including 130 million migrant workers. Such population mobility was caused mainly due to the imbalance between urban and rural areas in terms of employment, income and living standards. Globally, population mobility, particularly migration, is a complex and important issue concerning economic and social development. Generally, people from underdeveloped countries with lower living standards prefer migration to developed economies with higher living standards.

To summarize, in the era of deepening globalization full of challenges and opportunities for future development, different countries still vary greatly in development levels. Cultural diversity still exists as countries at different stages of development naturally adopt different strategies and initiatives for their own economic and social development. Therefore, to achieve sustainable and stable economic development throughout the world, it is necessary to establish effective systems and mechanisms for achieving State-to-State coordinated inclusive and institutional arrangements. In order to realize the sustainable development of economy and society, it is necessary to establish effective systems and mechanisms to achieve balance between humans and nature, and between the economy and nature. This requires not only the efforts of developing countries, but also those developed countries. In exploring new development modes, both sides face common tasks. In order to build a harmonious and stable happy society, at a time when globalization and cultural diversity prevail, it is necessary to establish an effective system and mechanism to achieve inclusion among different social strata.

6.2 Rural Development as Fundamental to Inclusive Development

6.2.1 Origin and Meaning of Inclusive Development

In 2007, the Asian Development Bank first proposed the concept of "inclusive growth". Effective inclusive growth must focus on high growth conducive to creating productive job opportunities, and social inclusiveness helping to ensure equality in opportunities and reduce risks, especially through a social security network benefiting vulnerable groups. This seeks coordinated and sustainable development of society and the economy, rather than pure economic growth. The term "inclusiveness" was proposed in the U.N. Millennium Development Goals. At the Boao Forum for Asia held on April 15, 2011, former Chinese President Hu Jintao delivered a keynote speech entitled *Inclusive Development: Common Agenda and New Challenges*, emphasizing that inclusive development would ensure globalization, regional economic integration and economic growth benefit everyone, particularly disadvantaged groups and the less developed countries. Growth generally refers to economic growth, while development has a broader meaning, covering economic and social sectors, including the relationship between humans and nature.

The concept of "inclusive development" was proposed to cope with the status quo of economic and social development and the prominent problems hindering global development. Internationally, since the end of the Cold War, the world has achieved long-term, stable development. In particular, globalization has achieved in-depth development greatly benefiting the developed countries. At the same time, developing countries, especially the emerging ones, have greatly improved their economic strength in the process of globalization, with profound changes in international economic strength comparisons and the relationship of rights and interests. Such changes have been impacting the international economic system and operating mechanism formed since the end of World War II. As we know, two cruel world wars in the last century created an abyss of human misery. Can human beings have enough wisdom and ability to find a path to peaceful, coordinated and joint development on the basis of rationally identifying differences and real changes? This is a problem urgently needing solution.

With the constant increase in global population, the current mode of economic and social development based on consumption of fossil energy and natural resources, seems increasingly out of date because environmental pollution and destruction arising therefrom have been greatly aggravated, which is generally recognized by the international community. More greenhouse gas emissions, constant global warming and more extreme climate disasters mean urgent positive international action is needed, including energy conservation and emission reduction, to ultimately realize green development and achieve harmony between humans and nature.

Almost all countries have encountered a number of prominent social problems since the 2008 international financial crisis. From the perspective of social development, various countries have faced fresh vulnerability. For example, after the international financial crisis, widespread wealth inequality and poverty problems emerged in more countries; employment difficulties and high unemployment problems were exacerbated; and more severe problems related to agriculture, rural areas and farmers, and food security problems appeared in developing countries; the problem of population aging in developed countries became acute; an obvious problem of high welfare exceeding the economic support capacity gripped some developed countries. In the U.S., the world's largest economy, the richest people (1% of total population) hold more than 40% of total national wealth, while the poorest group (80% of total population) owns only 17%. This is the most unequal level of wealth distribution since the 1920s. In 2010, the number of impoverished Americans reached 46.2 million, a new high in the past fifty-two years. The world is facing challenges to solve the longstanding social problems as new ones emerge. The situation is similar in China. It has greatly improved overall living standards, social security and social services. However, the income distribution gap in society among various social members, social classes, employees in different industries and regions has greatly expanded. The gap between the rights and interests of different social members in the possession or usage of resources has greatly widened. Based on a poverty line of RMB2,300, China still has 128 million people below this level. The low living standard of farmers, the Gini coefficient of rural areas being close to the international warning line, and the expansion of the income gap between farmers and urban citizens are typical manifestations of uneven income distribution. In the face of many problems and social contradictions, including the enlarged income gap and uneven resource ownership, we are shouldering a heavy task to maintain social stability and realize new development.

At present, human beings encounter a number of major problems in the process of pursuing development and a better life. These are usually caused or accumulated in the development process, and can be solved only by further development, because there is no eternal solution in the world. This is the historical origin of inclusive development. That is to say, we need to use inclusive ideas and methods to realize inclusiveness between countries and between humans and nature, and social inclusion, so as to achieve new development. This is also a strategic way to achieve sustainable development.

6.2.2 *Worldwide Issues of Agriculture, Rural Areas and Farmers*

In essence, issues of agriculture, rural areas and farmers refer to the imbalance between agriculture and nonfarm sectors, between rural and urban areas, and between farmers and citizens at large, as well as relative weakness of agriculture, rural areas and farmers.

China is undergoing rapid industrialization and urbanization. However, the issues of agriculture, rural areas and farmers have become more prominent in the process. Agriculture is a typical weak industry. In 2011, the added value of the primary industry was RMB4,771.2 billion, accounting for 10.1% of GDP; about three hundred million people were employed by the sector, accounting for 35% of total employment; the agricultural mechanization level had achieved a penetration rate of 54.5%. From this we see that China's agriculture is still weak, with low labor productivity, high labor intensity and high risk. The agricultural working population is inferior to its nonfarm equivalent in terms of scientific and cultural quality and in its age profile. In 2011, China entered an era of urbanization, with an urbanization rate of 51.27% comprising 691 million people. There still remained a rural population of 657 million distributed over about 41,000 towns and 620,000 administrative villages. Although the rural population was less than the urban one, the proportion of rural working group in the total population of the countryside was 53%, which is higher than that in urban areas. The problem of the urban-rural dual structure remains prominent. Compared with urban communities, their rural equivalents are less modernized and lag far behind in living quality, living environment, development opportunities and availability of public services. Rural areas are far behind in terms of structural reform, and market-oriented reform of land and water resources, real estate and infrastructure, thus offering limited attraction to modern factors of economic and social development. In contrast with urban areas that are experiencing rapid growth, rural areas face a very grim developmental situation. Farmers, as relatively vulnerable groups, enjoy far less income, public services and development opportunities than urban residents. In 2011, the per capita net income of farmers was RMB6,977, creating a ratio of 1:3.23 when set against the per capita urban disposable income. We face a very tough task to achieve a relatively balanced and stable increase of urban and rural incomes.

In the process of industrialization and urbanization, developing countries generally encounter prominent problems related to agriculture, rural areas and farmers. Such problems also exist in some developed countries, constituting an important part of relative economic, social, and political backwardness. Developed countries usually adopt an agricultural subsidy policy, indicating their farming sector is less competitive. Despite modernization, developed countries have not completely changed the mode of seasonal agricultural production and a management system highly sensitive to natural changes. Despite the rapid progress of science and technology, accelerated development of industries, particularly high-tech ones, continuous improvement in wealth creation efficiency, and diversity of urban living and development opportunities, rural communities are facing new challenges in regard to construction and development.

6.2.3 Strategically Addressing the Issues of Agriculture, Rural Areas and Farmers for Inclusive Development

In essence, inclusive development refers to the coordinated and fair advancement of the economy and society involving different groups and countries, and also harmony between humans and nature. Inclusive development should benefit a wide range of different parties, particularly vulnerable groups, on the principle of fairness, justice and equality. "Inclusive development" embodies such a concept, and so, China decided to adopt this strategy in line with the its own situation. It is not only of great significance to solve a series of major problems currently being faced, but also a strategic measure to innovate the developmental concept of and fully embrace a commitment to achieving sustainable development.

Undergoing rapid growth in the period of some thirty years since the reform and opening up begun in late 1978, China has entered a critical phase in building a moderately prosperous society in all aspects. According to the International Monetary Fund (IFM), China ranked 90th in the world in 2011, with per capita GDP of USD5,414, representing a middle-income level or above. Countries reaching this stage have to overcome the "middle-income trap", so as to become high-income ones. According to international experience, a country with a per capita GDP of less than USD1,000 will encounter a development "trap"; a country at the stage of economic take-off usually has a per capita GDP of USD1,000–3,000; a country with the per capita GDP in the range of USD3,000–10,000 must address various economic and social contradictions and complete tough structural adjustment and development mode transformation to achieve new development. China has entered a period of transition from an upper-middle-income country to a high-income one, undergoing significant changes in its domestic situation, the range of development tasks, development goals, development constraints and external environmental risks than those experienced thirty years ago. In the era of globalization, a favorable and peaceful international environment is needed to promote new, inclusive development in many countries. China should solve the aforesaid problems of uneven wealth distribution and imbalanced development and undertake institutional innovations, to achieve inclusive development based on fairness, justice and equal opportunities. We should focus on energy conservation and emissions reduction, strengthen independent innovation and accelerate transformation of economic development modes, while continuing to introduce advanced technologies from other countries, to truly achieve green, balanced and inclusive development between the economy and society and between humans and nature.

The biggest challenge for inclusive development in national and social development lies in the development of agriculture, rural areas, and farmers. Weak agriculture, large but underdeveloped rural areas, and massive but vulnerable farming communities are both the difficulties and priorities for achieving inclusive development. The imbalance between the agricultural and nonfarm sectors, between rural areas and urban areas, and between farmers and the broader community, still dominates, which must be addressed to achieve national economic and social development. The largest difficulty of building a moderately prosperous society in all aspects comes from rural areas.

6.3 Strengthening Technical Innovations, Accelerating Rural Development, and Promoting Inclusive Development

Inclusive development rests strongly with the development of agriculture, rural areas and farmers. For the nonfarm sectors and cities and towns, where citizens enjoy favorable development conditions and high starting points in achieving fast development, the key for inclusive development is making breakthroughs in systems and mechanisms, so as to achieve overall, fast, balanced and inclusive development that gradually reduces the gap between different sectors, between rural and urban areas, and between farmers and urban citizens.

6.3.1 Innovations Promoting and Accelerating Inclusive Development of Rural Areas

The primary task of rural development is promoting advanced agriculture. To achieve national inclusive development, it is necessary to accelerate agricultural development rather than restricting nonfarm development. Traditional agriculture has lower labor productivity than that of nonfarm sectors, and such features as seasonal production, sensitivity to natural risks, poor scale expansion and profitability, create disadvantages in attracting talents, technologies, investment and other factors extremely important for agricultural development. To accelerate the latter, we must fundamentally undertake strategic adjustments to the agricultural structure and development modes, accelerate the output of technologies, talents and investments, build a modern agricultural industry, promote creation of an industrial chain, develop the sectors' profitability, competitiveness and attractiveness to modern industry factors, so as to narrow the gap between agricultural and nonfarm sectors. To this end, innovations are required. The practices of the U.S., Israel, Canada, Australia, Netherlands and other countries, all with the most advanced modern agriculture, prove that traditional agriculture can become an internationally competitive modern industry. China's agriculture has typical features such as insufficiency of natural resources, and low levels of technology and marketization. China, a large country with huge population, must independently solve its food security problems. We must rely on technical innovations to overcome the constraints of insufficient natural resources, guide the flow of non-natural resources to the agricultural sector under government guidance, and make the same competition and development opportunities available to agriculture, to substantially improve labor productivity.

To achieve comprehensive development of rural areas, it is necessary to develop modern agriculture and vigorously build modern rural communities and a harmonious rural society. At present, as noted, China's urbanization level is 51.3%, which is the global average, but lower than the 70% average level of developed countries. Even if the urbanization level of China reaches that level, there will still be more than four hundred million farmers in China. Nowadays, nearly seven hundred million farmers live in about 620,000 administrative villages widely distributed in China, who must be included to truly build a moderately prosperous society in all aspects and realize modernization. The realistic solution is to build modern rural communities where people can live a modern life. Due to a huge development gap between urban and rural areas, more resources and elements are seen in the former. We must explore new paths to accelerate rural development, and an innovation-driven approach is the best choice. For a long time, a village has usually been regarded as a place of residence, and related policies are available not for community development and management. Rural areas lag behind urban areas in the degree of reform and development, and formulation of corresponding laws, regulations and policies for economic development. For example, rural areas are extremely weak in marketized applications and management of natural resources such as land, real estate and public facilities, and seriously lag behind in development of property rights. Urban and rural areas are quite different, forming the typical urban-rural dual structure. To accelerate inclusive development of rural areas, we must give them the same development opportunities, promote reform and opening up using scientific concepts and methods for urban-rural integration, break down barriers in laws and policies, guide the flow of modern economic and social development elements to rural areas, and further narrow the urban-rural gap.

The problem of farmers finds expression chiefly in the development gap between them and other citizens. Personal development is the ultimate goal of development. In China, human development has to include everyone. As the country has entered a critical period of building a moderately prosperous society in all aspects, transitioning from an upper-middle-income country to a high-income one, with rapid industrialization and urbanization, it is an urgent task to solve the development problems of farmers through delivery of jobs, medical resources, public services, education, training and other opportunities. According to the requirements of urban-rural integration, the first priority is to enable farmers to enjoy the same development opportunities as everyone else. At the same time, relevant systems involving farmer management and services should also be reformed, with efforts to break down the urban-rural dual structure to achieve full integration. As an outcome of this structure, the problem of migrant workers in China relates to management of both urban and rural areas. To achieve inclusive development and accelerate rural development, we must give priority to narrowing gaps between different groups.

6.3.2 Priorities of Rural Technical Innovation

To accelerate the inclusive development of agriculture, rural areas and farmers through technical innovation, we must clarify the priorities involved based on national conditions and challenges at the present stage.

(1) Strengthening technical studies of agriculture and rural areas

First, we should strengthen basic research on the construction and development of modern agriculture, the rural economy and society, and rural communities. The particularity of China's agriculture, rural areas and farmers' problems determines a number of basic and theoretical issues needing in-depth study. It is worth noting we have undertaken more research on agricultural production, but less on the agricultural industrial chain, especially on agricultural product innovation, logistics, market management and other issues, and this has to change.

The rural economy is the material foundation of rural development, backed by rural industries. We urgently need to eliminate limitations in thinking on the traditional agricultural economy, comprehensively study the issues of rural economic development, completely eradicate dual structure barriers to integrated development of urban and rural areas, create an environment in which economic factors all have equal opportunities to flow in an accelerated way to rural areas through innovations under government guidance, speed up the development of the rural economy, and focus on building a number of modern rural communities.

Rural society is an important carrier of Chinese traditional culture. Construction of a modern country needs modern social management, and rural society is the difficulty. Research of rural society is of great theoretical and scientific significance in constructing modern communities.

Second, we need more research into technical innovation to guide and support development of rural industries and the rural economy, community construction and social management. The interface whereby science serves the economy and society is the product and its supporting technology. Scientific and technological innovation serves inclusive development. What is vital is to make a breakthrough in product creation and the supporting production or management technology. Only by making such breakthroughs in product development and innovation is it possible for technology to link with enterprises and become the actual force of technological progress.

(2) Strengthening the transformation and industrialization of scientific and technological achievements related to agriculture and rural areas

First of all, we must attach great importance to the transformation of scientific and technological achievements related to agriculture and rural areas, which have strong regional characteristics. Compared with general industrial scientific and technological achievements, pilot regional tests and maturation of scientific and technological achievements related to agriculture and rural areas are crucial. The transformation of scientific and technological achievements related to agriculture and rural areas is indispensable, but is a weak link, so we must strengthen the transformation of scientific and technological achievements accordingly.

Second, we need to promote the industrialization of scientific and technological achievements on the basis of better protecting agricultural intellectual property rights. At present, technical innovation is weak in such protection and management. In consideration of the weakness of agriculture and the importance of food security, the government has always focused on supporting agricultural development through various protection measures. The widely recognized public welfare of agriculture weakens its marketability. Without the market and enterprises, there would be no modern agricultural industry. In order to give full play to the role of scientific and technological innovation, develop modern agriculture and build advanced rural communities, it is necessary to recognize and protect intellectual property rights. This is the only way to provide a strong connection with investment and the market, and realize sound development of industrialization. Effective protection of intellectual property rights can mobilize the enthusiasm of enterprises for technological innovation.

(3) Strengthening the promotion of agricultural and rural technologies and the popularization of scientific and technological knowledge

China's agriculture features relatively low organizational degree, small land scale and low marketization level. As a result, more than two hundred million farmers remain as agricultural producers without economic legal person status. Farmers' production activities are an important foundation for agricultural development. It is necessary to do a good job in scientific and technological services for farmers, public welfare scientific and technological services for agriculture, and strengthen the promotion of public agricultural science and technology in rural areas. China has established an agricultural technology application system covering the whole country, and has taken main responsibility of public technology promotion. The challenge is to establish and improve a dynamic operation mechanism to meet the needs of modern agricultural development and rural communities.

The popularization of scientific and technological knowledge in rural areas is a public welfare undertaking that must be constantly advanced to improve their scientific and technological level. Compared with urban areas, those in the countryside acquire knowledge through very limited channels, requiring more efforts to popularize scientific and technological knowledge. There should be equal opportunities for everyone to gain knowledge without which inclusive development will be hard to achieve. Therefore, we must take effective measures to strengthen the popularization of scientific and technological knowledge in rural areas to eliminate this weakness.

(4) Strengthening agricultural and rural innovations

Agricultural and rural innovation capacity construction is an important part of the national drive in this regard, and is the basis of implementing the strategy of relying on scientific and technological innovation for the full development of agricultural and rural areas.

First, we should continue to strengthen the capacity-building of basic agricultural and rural research in rural areas, mainly through universities and scientific research institutes, and to carry research on agricultural and rural issues.

Second, we will focus on cultivating and improving the technical innovation capacity of enterprises while strengthening agricultural and rural innovation capacity building. Enterprises have become the main force of agricultural product development, rural construction and development of rural industries. However, agriculture-related enterprises generally have weak technical innovation capacity, usually suffering from shortage of research and development institutions. Technical innovation capacity building is the key for enterprises to implement the technical innovation strategy. We should promote enterprises with large scale and good conditions to establish their own R&D institutions, and increase financial input into their work, so as to strengthen their R&D teams with a reasonable structure. For small-scale enterprises, we should promote the combination of production, teaching and research, strengthen the technical services of universities and scientific research institutions, and encourage enterprises to embrace innovation driven development.

Talents are most important in strengthening the innovation capacity building related to agriculture and rural areas. We should promote the training of all types of personnel by cultivating a large number of professional and technical talents, as well as agricultural entrepreneurs and experts in rural construction and management. To a certain extent, entrepreneurs and management experts are more important, as they are strategic talents able to set up enterprises, develop modern industries, manage and serve modern rural communities through integration of technology, land, labor force, investment and other factors.

(5) Strategic task of agricultural and rural entrepreneurship

The low level of agricultural industrialization, underdevelopment of rural industries, few employment opportunities, and heavy employment tasks have seriously hindered rural economic and social development. However, we can solve such problems by promoting technical entrepreneurship. In developed countries, entrepreneurship is of great concern for both governments and society. Since the reform and opening up, particularly since start of market economy construction, China has gradually paid more attention to entrepreneurship. Analysis shows entrepreneurship is mainly an urban activity. There are about 250 million farmer-turned workers in China, and also a large number of underemployed people in rural areas. For a large number of rural laborers, it is not advisable to simply adopt the strategy of entering the cities and towns to seek employment. The proper solution is to develop urban and rural overall planning simultaneously. On the one hand, efforts could be undertaken to create conditions to expand employment, to attract rural population to settle in cities. On the other hand, we must start and strengthen rural entrepreneurship to enable farmers to find jobs locally.

Promoting rural entrepreneurship is of strategic significance for the development of agriculture and the rural areas in general. On the one hand, the start-up of rural entrepreneurship work will vigorously promote the adjustment of the concept of agricultural and rural development through entrepreneurship. For this, it is necessary to give priority to the flow of industrial development elements to the city, while the vast rural areas, lagging behind in development and in urgent need of this element, can still play a prominent role of "the rural areas supporting the cities". By supporting entrepreneurship, talents, science and technology and investment will then be lured into the rural areas. We have made efforts to change the historical "urban-rural dual structure" that hindered rural economic development. However, we also need to give full play to the role of the market mechanism to promote development of agricultural and rural economy. While giving full play to the government's support for the development of agriculture and rural areas, we should also use the regulatory role of the market mechanism in accordance with the institutional and policy arrangements of urban-rural integration to realize the flow of industrial elements to the countryside, provide a good and healthy development environment for rural industry and economic development, thus addressing the weak links of market mechanism in the development of rural areas.

Here is a typical case in point. In 2002, the Ministry of Science and Technology initiated pilot work of special commissioners in science and technology in rural areas, combining entrepreneurial talents with investment, rural natural resources, markets, information and other industrial development elements in accordance with market rules to set up communities of shared interests to collaborate with farmers. Entrepreneurial talents include those who are good at the circulation and processing of agricultural products, or scientific and technological talents or those adept in management. Most importantly, such talents must have entrepreneurial abilities. In essence, a community of shared interests can also be an enterprise, a cooperative, or an association. Its essence is a legal entity sharing interests and risks. By 2011, the number of science and technology special commissioners had increased to 170,000. Through the special commissioners' entrepreneurial activities, more than 8,300 enterprises were founded, attracting more than RMB4 billion of bank loans, making it possible for about fifty million farmers to participate in entrepreneurship. It made a remarkable contribution to rural industry.

6.3.3 Policy Suggestions

Since the international financial crisis of 2008, the world has been facing the heavy task of restoring economic growth, and the challenge of addressing global climate change, reducing poverty and developing a green economy. On this planet with a large population, adopting inclusive development is a strategic choice for seeking common ground while reserving differences, so as to enjoy common, peaceful and harmonious development. The issues of agriculture, rural areas, and farmers are the primary issues confronting development in China needing to be addressed for realization of a well-off society. Similar problems widely exist in developing countries, and they even exist in developed countries, closely related to poverty. As far as China is concerned, the key to success is to achieve inclusive development of the agriculture and non-agriculture sectors, rural and urban areas. An important measure is to speed up the development of agriculture, rural areas and farmers through scientific and technological innovation so that the inclusive development strategy can be turned into practical action.

(1) Making the rural technical innovation strategy for inclusive development

The issues of agriculture, rural areas and farmers concern national economic and social development. Scientific and technological innovation should be taken as a strategic measure to change the mode of development, accelerate development and lead structural adjustment. It is necessary for the central government to formulate an overall rural technical innovation strategy for inclusive development. The strategy involves development of agriculture and farmers, rural community construction and management, rural income distribution, poverty alleviation, public services, ecological environment construction, institutional reform and innovation in urban-rural integration, and other deep-seated issues. The government and all sectors of society should reach a consensus on such a strategy, the development goals, important tasks and major measures to be undertaken, to form a strategic deployment, making innovation the leading factor to accelerate the development of agriculture, rural areas and farmers, and realizing the inclusive development for everyone.

(2) Seeking innovative development of agriculture, rural areas and farmers

An institutional guarantee is required for inclusive development. First, we should have the system that can effectively eliminate the "urban-rural dual structure". Urban and rural communities should come under unified management so as to create effective urban-rural governance. Second, there should be a system for farmers to enjoy equal opportunities for the development with the rest of society, including equal opportunities in the fields of employment, public services, education, medical care, and so on. The unequal possession of assets between farmers and the rest of society is an important aspect of the difference in development opportunities between farmers and citizens. In the vast rural areas, the current land use policies put farmers in a very unfavorable position, so reform should be carried out as soon as possible. Third, integration is required in the industrial development environment. The key is to establish the basic role of the market mechanism in the allocation of industrial development elements in rural areas, break through the bottleneck of rural property rights, especially land capitalization, and realize the free flow of industrial development elements in urban and rural areas. It is also the key to introducing investment, science and technology and other modern industrial development elements into the countryside and accelerating the development of agriculture and rural areas.

(3) Policies to support rural innovation and entrepreneurship

First, we need to improve the policies that support rural innovations, including those that increase investment in agricultural R&D, and the transformation and extension of agricultural scientific and technological research fruits, as well as improving agricultural technical innovation capabilities. In terms of the design of policies, it is necessary to focus on solving the problems plaguing enterprises with weaknesses in this regard. It is vital that industrial enterprises should rely on scientific and technological innovation to realize their own long-term development, and so there should be policies in place to specifically encourage and support them. Second, there should be policies that support rural entrepreneurship. In view of a huge gap between rural and urban areas in terms of the development environment and conditions, central and local governments should formulate corresponding fiscal taxation, financial and social capital investment policies that can encourage, support and serve rural entrepreneurship to reduce costs and risks. Efforts should be made to deepen reforms, overcome institutional constraints on the flow of industrial elements, and give full play to the role of market regulation, so as to create a favorable environment for rural entrepreneurship.

(4) Strengthen talent cultivation

To achieve inclusive development, we should make necessary adjustments to policies related to talent cultivation for rural development. At present, professionals of agriculture and forestry are mainly cultivated in some specialized universities and vocational colleges. Due to historical reasons, these usually focus on research and teaching on agricultural production, paying little attention to post-harvest links extremely important for the development of a modern agricultural sector, particularly market management. Little work is undertaken in talent cultivation specifically for better construction and management of rural communities. To develop modern agriculture, build modern rural communities, and cultivate new-type farmers, we need a large number of talents with skills in industrial management and business operation, professionals familiar with modern agriculture, particularly the agricultural industry chain, and also those with local knowledge. In deepening the reform of universities and vocational training institutions, we should continue to do a good job of cultivating professional talents, and, at the same time, work hard to promote the merger of science and engineering and social disciplines, and vigorously strengthen the cultivation of composite talents that meet the needs of the development of modern agriculture and rural communities.

(5) Improving financial policies conducive to development of rural industries

The development of modern rural industries is inseparable from financial involvement; they cannot rely on petty loans alone. Compared with urban industries, rural industries have obvious disadvantages in attracting financial investments for many reasons: First, rural industries are underdeveloped and of low-level as a whole. For a long time, agriculture has remained the most important industrial sector in rural areas, while other industries are underdeveloped. Rural industries focus on agricultural planting, livestock breeding and other production links, with little consideration of post-production storage, logistics, wholesale and terminal marketing. Existing enterprises in rural areas are generally of small scale and short of talents with low technical level. Second, rural industries have poor development conditions, and low degree of marketization in land use and asset management, lagging behind in the property aspects of assets in the legal sense. Compared to urban areas, rural areas face a wealth of difficulties in development of a real estate industry. Third, there are few specialized financial instruments for the development of rural industries. For example, rural entrepreneurship requires specialized financial instruments for venture investment, insurance and investment exit. To expand and strengthen rural industry, it is necessary to have bank credit, social investment and arrangements for docking with the capital market in line with the characteristics of the rural industry.

To solve the problem of insufficient funds for rural development, we must make systematic arrangements in industrial and financial policies. In encouraging the development of rural industries, we need to support the local areas so as to provide a wealth of loan recipients for financial investment. At the same time, we need to undertake research into and form specialized financial instruments that meet the requirements of rural industry and rural entrepreneurship development.

China is entering a critical period of building a moderately prosperous society in all aspects and achieving the transition from an upper-middle income country to a higher-income one. In the past thirty years or so, China has experienced sustained and rapid growth, and undergone tremendous changes in economic and social development, and made great achievements in poverty alleviation. Tremendous changes come up concerning the country's external environment. During the period, traditional development modes have faced severe pressure for change forcing China to seek a breakthrough in exploring effective modes of green, sustainable development, which is a major task for China and a common responsibility for the whole world. Inclusive development calls on the fruits of globalization and economic development benefit all countries and regions and their entire population. Efforts have to be made to achieve green and sustainable development. In the near future, inclusive development definitely will receive more attention, and more research and related work will be carried out for this purpose. This will play a significant role in promoting the development of agriculture, rural areas and farmers.

Chapter 7
Promoting Inclusive Development with More Effective Environmental Policies

Lizhi Zhu, Zhenbin Gu, and Dandan Huang

7.1 Ecologically Vulnerability and Poverty: Breaking the Vicious Cycle

Ecologically vulnerable areas refer to the transitional ones between two different types of ecosystems and being a focus of ecological protection. In such areas, the ecological system is unstable and unbalanced, with weak ability to cope with interference, while the ecological carrying capacity is low. They are, therefore exposed to sabotage and need special protection. In this chapter, the ecologically vulnerable areas refer to those where changes in the ecological environment or human production and lifestyle will cause an obvious decline in land productivity or even total disappearance (Chen 2008). China's ecologically vulnerable areas are mainly found in the arid and semi-arid parts of the north, hilly regions in the south, the mountains in the southwest, the Qinghai-Tibet Plateau and the eastern coastal region (Ministry of Ecology and Environment 2008). Highly overlapping with contiguous impoverished regions, the ecologically vulnerable areas tend to have high concentrations of poverty, hence becoming target areas of poverty alleviation. Exposed to frequent natural disasters, these areas have insufficient capacity in disaster prevention and resistance, and low carrying capacity for economic growth and social development, resulting a tough task of reducing and getting rid of poverty.

L. Zhu · Z. Gu · D. Huang (✉)
Institute of Agricultural Economics and Development, Chinese Academy of Agricultural Sciences, Beijing, China
e-mail: zhulz@mail.caas.net.cn

C. Zuo et al. (eds.), *Inclusive Development and Poverty Reduction*,
International Research on Poverty Reduction,
https://doi.org/10.1007/978-981-15-8446-6_7

7.1.1 Poverty Mainly Occurs in Ecologically Vulnerable Areas

From the founding of the People's Republic of China in 1949 to the early days of reform and opening up begun in late 1978, poverty was a common phenomenon. Driven by a series of reform measures such as the household responsibility system, however, the rural economy has developed rapidly and poverty has been greatly mitigated. However, some areas are still unable to get rid of poverty or even maintain the most basic needs for existence. With the gradual reduction of the impoverished population and the increasingly obvious regional characteristics of poverty, the problem in ecologically vulnerable areas then attracted widespread attention. A study published at the end of the 20th Century showed that about 75.92% of the counties in the ecologically vulnerable areas were classified as impoverished ones, containing about 43.33% of the land area, 67.96% of the cultivated land and 75.86% of the population (Zhou and Ruomei 1994). It is clear that China's poverty problem is highly related to fragile ecological environment. The poverty-stricken population in ecologically vulnerable areas is relatively concentrated.

In recent years, with the deepening of rural reform and the increasing efforts of poverty alleviation, the geographical characteristics of the distribution of the poor have become increasingly obvious. China's poverty-stricken population mainly live in the deep mountains, stone mountains, deserts, alpine areas, the Loess Plateau, the reservoir areas, and areas with high incidence of endemic diseases in the central and western China. Most of them are the old revolutionary base areas, the border areas and areas inhabited by ethnic minorities. In 2009, the monitoring of the National Bureau of Statistics showed that 65.9% of the country's poor people lived in the western region; the incidence of poverty in the eastern, central and western regions was 0.5%, 3.3% and 8.3% respectively, among which the five provinces of Guizhou, Yunnan, Shaanxi, Gansu and Qinghai, and the two autonomous regions of Tibet and Xinjiang saw higher incidence of poverty (all over 5%). Obviously, these are the ecologically vulnerable areas sharing the same characteristics: remote location, inconvenient infrastructure, ecological imbalances, slow economic development and underdeveloped culture and education. It is difficult for people and animals there to have access to drinking water, and the production and living conditions are extremely poor.

7.1.2 The Great Difficulties of Poverty Alleviation in the Ecologically Vulnerable Areas

It is generally believed that there is a law of diminishing marginal utility in the poverty reduction effect of economic growth which means, when the incidence of absolute poverty falls to a very low level, the role of economic growth in poverty reduction will gradually decline. If the government neither implements more targeted policies and measures nor changes the way of poverty alleviation, poverty reduction will significantly slow down its pace and slipping back into poverty will occur in a large scale. After its achievements of poverty alleviation have won high praises from the international community, China is facing the risks of declining efficiency of poverty alleviation, increasing difficulty of poverty reduction and more re-occurrence of poverty. The ecologically vulnerable areas, in particular, have great difficulties in coping with the contradiction between environmental protection and human survival and development. Therefore, it is difficult to balance poverty reduction and ecological improvement there. Moreover, the poverty alleviation and development aimed at increasing income will inevitably cause greater pressure on the resources and environment, which may lead to the destruction of the ecological environment, and even further aggravate the poverty in the ecologically vulnerable areas. As the sustainable development of economy and society is constrained by resources and environment, the goal of poverty reduction and ecological improvement must be taken into account, which is the root cause of the increasing difficulty of poverty reduction in ecologically vulnerable areas.

7.1.3 Ecologically Vulnerable Areas Can Hardly Consolidate the Achievements of Poverty Reduction

There is a distinct phenomenon in which people who have been lifted out of poverty fall back into poverty. In 2003, the number of people living in absolute poverty in China increased by 800,000, which led to not only skepticism about the effectiveness of poverty alleviation efforts but also concerns about the problem of people falling back into poverty. In fact, such relapse is not uncommon in the process of fighting against poverty. Especially, the ecologically vulnerable areas where poor people have low development capacity and weak development foundation, tend to suffer from economic losses and poverty when there are external confounding factors such as natural disasters, ecological changes and market risks (Yan 2005).

Natural disaster is the major cause of the massive re-occurrence of poverty. High rates of natural disasters are also found in the ecologically vulnerable areas. On the one hand, agriculture and animal husbandry are the leading industries in poor areas. They are dependent most on natural conditions and most directly damaged by natural disasters. It is easy for them to suffer from economic losses when natural disaster happens. China is one of the countries with the most severe damages caused by natural disasters in the world. In the ecologically vulnerable areas in western China, natural disasters keep occurring with weak prevention and resistance ability. It is very hard to consolidate the fruits of poverty alleviation in these areas. On the other hand, casualties in natural disasters are inevitable. Families affected by natural disasters fall into absolute poverty due to injuries, diseases or labor reduction, which will make the follow-up efforts in poverty alleviation more difficult. According to the combined consultation and analysis launched by the Ministry of Civil Affairs and other departments in 2011, all kinds of natural disasters across the country affected 430 million people, among whom 1,126 died (or disappeared). The direct economic loss was RMB309.64 billion. More than 80% of the dead (or missing), the relocated people and collapsed houses caused by disasters were distributed in the old revolutionary base areas, areas inhabited by minority nationalities, remote and border areas and poverty-stricken areas. The analysis also shows that the natural disasters in China in 2011 were less heavy compared with previous years. It can be deduced that natural disasters have seriously disturbed and damaged the efforts of poverty alleviation in China and it is very difficult to consolidate the fruits of poverty alleviation in the ecologically vulnerable areas.

7.1.4 Poverty and Environmental Degradation in Ecologically Vulnerable Areas Interact in Terms of Both Cause and Effect

At the United Nations Conference on Environment and Development in 1992, the representatives of the participating countries agreed: in the third world, poverty is the root cause of the environmental degradation of many developing countries and environmental degradation leads to further poverty in these countries. Such a vicious cycle has made developing countries face difficulties in environment and development (Wang 1993). In fact, the relationship between poverty and environmental degradation is not as simple as that. Taking one of the two as the inducement is not necessarily to form a vicious circle. The decisive factor behind it is the carrying capacity of regional natural resources to population, economy and social development. That is to say, when the carrying capacity of regional resources and environment to population, economy and social development is insufficient, poverty and environmental degradation will occur together and interact as both cause and effect for each other.

In the ecologically vulnerable areas, the causal relationship between poverty and ecological deterioration is very obvious. Take the arid and semi-arid areas in northern China as an example. Over-cultivation and over-grazing for the purpose of getting rid of poverty will inevitably lead to ecological damage. The resulting natural disasters will in turn aggravate poverty (or lead to re-occurrence of poverty). If the way of living that highly relies on natural resources can not be changed, poverty alleviation efforts in ecologically vulnerable areas are bound to impose greater pressure on the ecological environment and make it more vulnerable. In order to break this vicious circle, we must start with improving the regional ecological environment and the carrying capacity of regional resources and environment, so that the population in the ecologically vulnerable areas can benefit from the ecological governance in the long run.

7.2 Ecological Improvement and Poverty Alleviation in China: Achievements and Problems

Ever since the end of the 20th century, China has stepped up its efforts in ecological restoration and environmental protection. In terms of environmental issues such as water and soil erosion and land degradation that seriously affect the long-term sustainable development of economy and society, a number of eco-projects have been launched successively in the major ecological buffer zones, river sources and ecologically vulnerable areas. At present, most of these projects have gone through a construction cycle and achieved remarkable ecological, social and economic benefits. However, many problems remain there. This chapter summarizes and analyzes the issue from the perspective of ecological improvement and poverty alleviation.

7.2.1 Grain for Green Program

The program that was aimed at converting cropland to forest and grassland was officially launched in 2002 to mitigate soil erosion in key areas; it was unprecedent in terms of the amount of investment, the size of the area involved, the strength of government policy support and the degree of public involvement (Li 2009). The program would be rolled out in four distinct areas: the key water source conservation areas, those suffering from water and soil erosion on the Loess Plateau, severely rocky, desertified areas and key sandy areas. According to relevant regulations, the major task is to plant forests intended to serve ecological functions only, i.e., in which the commercial use of any wood, fuelwood and non-wood forest products is prohibited. These forests much make up no less than 80% of the selected area. The government would compensate, in both cash and kind, farmers enrolled in the program. The term limits for the compensation are: two years for those planting grass on land once used for crop cultivation, five years for those planting trees for commercial use of non-wood forest products, and eight years for those planting trees for ecological restoration only. The compensation package included 150 kg of coarse grain for program enrollees in the Yangtze River valley and areas to the south, 100 kg for enrollees in the Yellow River valley and areas to the north, plus RMB20 per mu per year, and RMB50 per mu in one-off subsidy for seedlings and afforestation work. In 2004, the in-kind component of the package was replaced by equivalent cash payment, at the rate of RMB1.4 for each kg of coarse grain. The compensation. In 2007, the central government extended cash compensation to those who stayed in the program. Enrollees in the Yangtze River valley and areas to the south would be eligible for RMB105 per mu, and those in the Yellow River valley and areas to the north would be eligible for RMB70 per mu. The additional RMB20 per year per mu living allowance subsidy remained the same. The term limits for the compensation were also unchanged: Two years for grass, five years for trees for commercial use of their non-wood forest products, and eight years for trees used exclusively for ecological restoration. By the end of 2010, the total area of land converted under the Grain for Green Program was 427 million mu (about 28.5 million ha) and the investment from the central government had topped RMB450 billion. All together 124 million farmers from 32 million rural households in the project areas benefitted. In the next phase of the program, in addition to making sure that achievements so far are sustained, afforestation would be carried out on land reclaimed for crop cultivation, as well as in other uncultivated areas, including mountainous regions, by imposing entry restrictions if necessary.

Since the implementation of the pilot project in 1999, overall progress has been smooth with remarkable results. Afforestation has been accelerated, the amount of vegetation has been increased, and the damage caused by soil erosion and sand storms has been mitigated; the direct subsidy policy under the forest and grassland rehabilitation programs has won widespread support from farmers. The grain subsidy and subsidy for living expenses constitute an important part of the income of farmers taking part in the project whose lives have been improved. However, we have still many problems in consolidating the fruits of project construction. First, compared with a series of policies to support agriculture, such as direct subsidies for grain producers, general subsidies for agricultural production supplies and subsidies for superior crop varieties, payments for converting cropland to forest and grassland have declined and will expire soon. Driven by a desire to pursue their own interests, farmers are very likely to resume cultivation on the land that has been converted to forest and grassland, creating fresh difficulties. Secondly, because of the extremely low profits yielded by the farmland converted, farmers are not greatly interested in making investment and engaging in management, and it is difficult for them to see any prospects of obtaining direct benefits from ecological improvement. Considering this, we must ensure that farmers can obtain long-term benefits from the project, and their income from converting land is higher than that from other methods of land utilization, if we are willing to continue the role of the project in improving ecology, reducing poverty and promoting social progress.

7.2.2 Rehabilitating Degraded Grassland with Grazing Ban

In 2003, China introduced grazing ban designed to address grassland degradation in five provinces—Gansu, Ningxia, Qinghai, Yunnan and Sichuan—and three autonomous regions—Inner Mongolia, Tibet and Xinjiang—and the Xinjiang Production and Construction Corps (XPCC). The program involves an array of measures designed to restore disturbed grassland ecosystems and strengthen the long-term economic value of the grasslands, and provides compensation to herders for lost earnings. These measures include building fences, reseeding, grazing ban, seasonal and rotational grazing, among others. Funding for the program came from the central government, local governments and farmers and herders. The central government partially subsidies fence construction and feed purchase; but herders practicing rotational grazing are not eligible for the feed subsidy. The amount of these subsidies depends on the type of grassland and the region involved. In the arid grassland in the western region of Inner Mongolia, Gansu and Ningxia region, degraded grasslands in eastern Inner Mongolia and northern Xinjiang, where grazing is prohibited year-round, herders receive compensation in the amount of 5.5 kg of feed grain per mu per year. For herders engaged in seasonal grazing, which by stipulation refers to grazing only during nine months each year, the compensation is 1.375 kg of feed grain per mu per year. The subsidy rate for fence construction is set at RMB16.5 per mu, 70% of which comes from the central government and 30% from local governments and individual herders; for herders in the river headwater areas in the east of the Qinghai-Tibet Plateau, where grazing is prohibited year-round, the central government offers 2.75 kg of feed grain per mu per year as compensation. Those engaged in seasonal grazing, which is grazing in only nine months each year, are eligible for 0.69 kg of grain for feed per mu per year. The subsidy rate for fence construction is set at RMB20 per mu, towards which the central government contributes 70%, and local governments and individual herders the other 30%. The feed grain subsidy would be in effect for five consecutive years. In 2011, the State Council made adjustments to the grazing ban, increasing the proportion of central government's contribution towards fence construction subsidy to 80%, or RMB20 per mu for the Qinghai-Tibet Plateau and RMB16 for other areas. Reseeding subsidy from the central government would reach RMB20 per mu. The central government provides RMB160 per mu in subsidy for grassland planted for purpose of feed production and RMB3,000 per household for subsidize shed construction.

Over the past 10 years, the grazing ban has largely worked as had been expected, meeting most targets and requirements. Thanks to the project, grassland degradation has largely been halted, and ecosystems notably rehabilitated. The project has earned praises from local governments and population for helping to transform the model of animal husbandry on grasslands and promoting economic development in these places. Monitoring shows that, in the project areas, the average vegetation coverage rate is 64%, which is 12% points higher than non-project areas; the grass height, fresh grass yield and fresh grazing grass yield are 21.3 cm, 3,185 kg per hectare and 2,713.5 kg per hectare respectively, which are 36.2%, 75.1% and 84.1% higher than that in non-project areas (Wang and Qiao 2011). However, several problems remain in policy implementation. First, the amount of the subsidies does not truly reflect the losses in earnings for the herders, which are in fact astronomical; secondly, measures currently in place cannot reverse the degradation of grassland caused by overgrazing, and they have made little difference to some of the most severely degraded grasslands. Therefore, unless we change the economic development model in these areas and wean the local population of their economic dependence on agriculture production and animal husbandry, grassland degradation would continue to worsen. And the eradication of poverty in the arid and semi-arid grassland areas in northern China would be unattainable.

7.2.3 Natural Forest Resources Protection Project

The Natural Forest Resources Protection Project (NFRPP) was officially launched in 2000, an important sign of the transformation of China's forestry sector from timber production to ecological construction. It is undertaken mainly to solve the problems of natural forest resources protection, regeneration, recovery and development in the upper reaches of the Yangtze River, the upper and middle reaches of the Yellow River, as well as the key state-owned forest areas in northeastern China, Inner Mongolia and other regions. Its main tasks are: Firstly, natural forest cutting is prohibited in the NFRPP region along the upper reaches of the Yangtze River and the upper and middle reaches of the Yellow River; timber production is reduced in the key state-owned forest areas of northeastern China and Inner Mongolia. Secondly, we should strictly manage and protect forest, shrubbery and young afforested land in the project area. Thirdly, the construction of forests for ecological benefits should be accelerated in the project area. After meeting the provisions of forest cutting prohibition and timber yield reduction, the most important problem in the project area includes the resettlement of surplus workers in forestry enterprises and social security issues. The surplus forestry workers have been given new jobs in the fields of forest management and protection and construction of forests for ecological benefits. The losses incurred to forestry workers, forestry companies and local governments due to the NFRPP Project have been compensated through social insurance and policy expenditure subsidies, and financial transfer payments. This highlights the fact that the NFRPP is not only the ecological construction project, but also the largest livelihood project involving forested areas. The second phase of NFRPP started in 2011 to undertake work not able to be completed in the first phase, and, at the same time, undertake the new task of realizing transformation of forest resources from restorative growth to improvement of forest quality. The purpose is to help the forest resources to be transformed from recovery growth to quality improvement and, through ecological construction and higher standards for project investment, create more job opportunities in forest areas, increase forestry workers' income, and improve the social security system for workers and residents of forest areas.

Smooth progress has been achieved in the first phase. The natural forest has been effectively protected and the ecological situation in the project area much improved; the forest industry has been increasingly optimized, people's livelihood improved with a harmonious and stable society; remarkable achievements have been recorded in forest industry enterprise reform. The NFRPP project has received good support from residents of the forestry areas. However, from the perspective of long-term sustainable development of the social economy in the NFRPP area, several problems remain in protecting the natural forest. Firstly, a long-term and stable investment mechanism and professional management and protection team are required to protect the natural forest serving as an ecological barrier. However, undertaking the NFRPP project is obviously a temporary measure. Secondly, the natural forest protection policy once directly caused poverty among the residents in the project area, and is obviously an important factor limiting economic and social development there.

How to coordinate ecological protection and economic development is still the core issue needing to be considered by the project managers. Apparently, if residents living in the project areas are limited in terms of their survival and development due to ecological protection measures, or they cannot obtain continuous benefits from ecological improvement, it will be very unfair on them and the project will not present a sustainable mode of ecological protection.

7.2.4 The Beijing-Tianjin Region Sandstorm Abatement Project

As a major part of the ecological improvement program for Beijing, Tianjin and the surrounding area, the project to control the sources of sandstorms in the region started in 2002. It is undertaken mainly to solve the problem of sandstorm hazards in the capital and its surrounding areas. According to the different causes of ecological problems in various areas, the project area is divided into four types (control areas): the desertification control area of the northern arid grassland, the Hunshandak Sandy Land control area, the control area of land desertification in the farming-pastoral ecotone area, and the Yanshan hilly and mountainous water source protection area. In accordance with the designation of these four types, we have taken targeted technical and controlling methods: First, this means strengthening pasture management and grassland construction. Efforts have been made to improve the grassland and the animal husbandry production mode to raise grassland productivity. Second, on the basis of protecting the existing forest and grass vegetation, efforts have been made to speed up pasture construction, expand forest and grass vegetation, fix sand dunes to curb their reactivation. Third, efforts have been made to prohibit reclamation and limit grazing to expand vegetation. More efforts have been made in closing off hillsides for afforestation, and speed up vegetation recovery. The policy of converting farmland to forest and grassland has been undertaken in areas with severe desertification. Fourth, the existing forest has been protected through closing hills or mountains. We have cultivated multi-layer forests for water and soil conservation, which combines arbor, shrub and grass in barren mountain and wasteland areas. Since 2011, the project has entered the stage of consolidating construction achievements. As various tasks are generally being promoted, we have worked on achieving better targeting in regard to the control areas and the way of vegetation recovery. During the 12th Five-Year Plan (2011–2015), the major tasks were set as to continuously implement the policy of returning farmland to forests (one of the remaining tasks from the first phase of the project), artificial afforestation, closing off hillsides for afforestation and aerial seeding.

In the past decade or so since the implementation of the project, the effect of sand control in the Beijing-Tianjin region and its surrounding areas has been truly remarkable. First, the ecological protection system in the region has assumed initial shape. The sandstorm situation changed from "going from bad to worse" to "being much improved". The results of grassland monitoring in 2010 show the vegetation coverage rate in the project area is 15% higher than that in the non-project area; secondly, days of sandy and dusty weather are obviously reduced and the ecological environment is greatly improved; third, the biodiversity index of the project area increased significantly, and the vegetation ecosystem has become more stable; fourth, the desertified land is obviously reduced, and the function of water and soil conservation is enhanced; and fifth, steady progress has been made in economic and social development and the capacity for sustainable development has been continuously enhanced. The contribution rate of project construction to regional sustainable development is being maintained in the range of 23.0% to 28.3%. Similar to the project of returning farmland to forest, the consolidation of the achievements of the project is also under pressure from policies that benefit farmers. Because the subsidy for returning farmland to forests is actually lower than the comprehensive income of grain production, farmers are more inclined to resume cultivation or increase livestock production. Therefore, ecological damage appears again in the project areas again. Obviously, the economic and social development of the project areas is still highly dependent on land, water and other natural resources. In order to promote economic growth, the way of resource utilization must follow the change of policies, which is the fundamental reason why ecological protection and construction projects are difficult to gain enduring support from farmers.

7.2.5 National Wildlife Protection and Construction of Nature Reserves

The project of wildlife protection and nature reserve construction started in 2001. It is a future—oriented and long-term ecological protection project with multiple strategic significance, aiming to solve the problems such as gene conservation, biodiversity protection, nature protection, and wetland protection. Major targets of the Overall Plan for the Construction of National Wildlife Protection and Nature Reserve Project are as follows: 15 rare and endangered wildlife species, including giant panda, red ibis, tiger, snub-nosed monkey, Tibetan antelope (Pantholopshodgsonii), Asian elephant, gibbon, musk deer, wild pheasant, cycads and orchid, will be saved; 40 kinds of wild animals and 120 kinds of wild plants of extreme rarity and among the most endangered species with destruction of their habitats will be saved and restored. Efforts are being made to strengthen in situ conservation, off-site conservation, and wild plant species conservation, and set free thirty species of captive wild animals and twenty species of rare wild plants. Efforts have also been made to strengthen scientific research on wildlife and wild plants, as well as species collection, conservation, saving and breeding; expand, improve and build a new batch of national nature reserves, game reserves, provenance bases and bases for breeding rare plants so as to restore and develop rare resources. A nature conservation network with international influence is expected to be formed finally, which takes natural reserves and important wetlands as the main contents, with reasonable layout, complete types, advanced facilities, and efficient management.

By the end of 2010, there were 2,035 forestry nature reserves nationwide, covering a total area of 124 million hectares, accounting for 12.89% of total national land; investment totals RMB5.928 billion, including RMB3.386 billion from the national government finance (State Forestry Administration 2011). With the implementation of the project, the conservation and breeding infrastructure for rare wild species such as red ibis and Chinese alligators, have been improved, leading to enhanced ability of wildlife rescue and breeding. The construction of the necessary infrastructure for the release of wild species has been promoted, with improved management ability in wildlife protection. Thus, some endangered wild animal species have enjoyed growth and expansion. Different from other ecological projects, the goal of wildlife protection and nature reserve construction project is relatively simple, aiming to protect rare wildlife species and their habitats rather than taking into account surrounding people's livelihood. In addition, with the increasing number of wild animal species, there are frequent incidents of crop damage and livestock casualties. At present, the compensation for farmers' losses is far from adequate, arousing complaints about the reserves among farmers.

In general, China's current ecological conservation and construction projects have played a crucial role in improving ecological environment. The policies of the project take into account both the objectives of regional poverty reduction and increasing farmers' income, and phased results have been achieved. However, in the long run, if we don't alter the backward development mode so highly reliant on natural resources in the ecologically vulnerable areas, and if people living in related regions cannot obtain continuous benefits from sustainable improvement of environment, the project will just be a short-term means to realize ecological protection and restoration. It will be hard to establish a long-term mechanism for such ecological improvement and poverty reduction.

7.3 Inclusive Development—Development Mode Combining Ecological Improvement with Poverty Reduction Goals

At present, China has found its efforts for ecological management and the eradication of poverty in ecologically vulnerable areas caught up in a conflict between the two, creating a dilemma of mutual restraint. On the one hand, China's impoverished people are mainly categorized under the heading of ecological poverty, which may only be eradicated if the ecological environment continues to improve. On the other hand, having achieved progress in the initial stage, the large-scale ecological construction projects supported by central finance are now facing severe challenges from livelihood issues. Local rural households would continue to destroy the environment for their own livelihood and development if they fail to gain continued investment from financial resources at all levels and be strictly bound by ecological protection policies. Therefore, ecological management and poverty reduction strategies in ecologically vulnerable areas of China have to be adjusted. Both goals need to be taken into account, and more importantly, they should coordinate and promote each other, turning from a vicious cycle to positive interaction. That means the inclusive development model should be explored for ecologically vulnerable areas, so that both ecological improvement and poverty reduction become the target of development in these areas, and the means to achieve sustainable social and economic development as well.

7.3.1 Meaning of Inclusive Development

As a mode of economic development proposed for poverty alleviation, inclusive development was first used by the Asian Development Bank, World Bank and other international agencies working to eliminate poverty, and then received attention from and became accepted by the governments of many developing countries. With the deepening of understanding of the relationship between economic growth, inequality and poverty alleviation, related research suggests intensifying inequality makes it hard for all people (especially the poor) to benefit from economic growth. And this is the root cause of economic growth failing to sustain efforts in poverty alleviation. Proposed as a countermeasure, inclusive development lays stress on building an inclusive system, providing a wide range of opportunities, eliminating the poverty of entitlement and social exclusion faced by the poor, achieving equal opportunities and fair participation for all. Its aim is to enable the impoverished population to participate in economic growth, making a contribution to it and properly sharing its fruits, like all other groups of the society, so as to realize the comprehensive development of each individual (Long Chaoyang 2012).

Equality of opportunity and sharing the results constitute the essence of inclusive development. Inclusiveness is a fundamental requirement for the process and results of economic growth. Specifically speaking, it has three clear senses. The first is to make economic growth to benefit all people, especially the poor. This is an important goal of inclusive development, and an essential condition for achieving sustained poverty reduction. The second is to offer everyone equal access to development opportunities. This provides the institutional guarantee for inclusive development, and also is the means to fully arouse the enthusiasm of all sectors of society and enhance the efficiency of economic growth. The third is to improve the individual ability to participate in the process of economic growth, and ensure the sustainability of poverty reduction.

7.3.2 Multi-objective Coordination Is the Essential Requirement of Inclusive Development

To realize the goal of poverty reduction for inclusive development, it is necessary to maintain rapid economic growth, reduce and eliminate inequality in enjoying opportunities in order to share the results of economic growth. In reality, however, it is difficult for economic growth to achieve efficiency while maintaining fairness and strike a balance between the two. Economic growth is the sole pre-requisite condition for poverty reduction. Eradication of poverty may sometimes be conflict with other goals of social development (such as ecological protection) in certain region where "inclusive development" needs to coordinate and realize multiple regional targets. In the first place, it is necessary to strike a balance among multi-targets to reduce conflicts and ensure their orderly realization; and then ensure measures targeting those targets complement each other in order to save social costs. It is thus clear that inclusive development serves to achieve sustainable socio-economic development with the lowest cost on the basis of striking a balance among various targets.

7.3.3 Inclusive Measures Are Required to Mitigate the Tension Between Ecological Improvement and Poverty Reduction

The above-mentioned analysis on achievements and problems of ecological projects in China show that, in China, ecological engineering is hard to carry on and ecological protection in ecologically vulnerable areas lacks a long-acting mechanism, the main reason lies in that residents in the project area cannot gain sustained benefit from ecological improvement; and backward development model featuring highly dependency on natural resources is the root cause of the difficulty in consolidating poverty reduction achievements in these areas. Ecological construction and poverty alleviation and development could not be sustained if there is a lack of external and continuously increasing investment (such as engineering investment, funds for poverty alleviation), because, in terms of the natural resources, a rivalry emerges between protection for ecological improvement and utilization for poverty reduction in these areas. Without effective coordination between the two goals, ecological improvement would bring about a constraint instead of being a driving force for regional economic growth, and further, exacerbate poverty.

To mitigate the tension between effort to improve ecological environment and effort to meet the goals of poverty reduction in the ecologically vulnerable areas, effort should be made to start from coordinating the relationship between resource protection and utilization. The concept of inclusive development should be used for reference and local residents should be offered equal opportunity to participate in ecological management, share the fruits of ecological management, or continue to benefit from the ecological improvement; and residents outside the project area should also be given reasonable compensation for their support to promote regional growth and so alleviate poverty. In fact, residents living in China's ecological project areas did not obtain the expected equal opportunity to participate in the construction. They only gained limited labor costs by undertaking simple work (such as subsidies from their returning farmland to forests, and from forest management and protection); their lost opportunities are not fully compensated. Therefore, we should look at China's ecological governance and poverty reduction strategies from a new perspective, and ensure they complement each other and thus form a virtuous circle by coordinating two strategic goals through institutional innovation.

7.4 Integrating Ecological Project and Poverty Reduction—Inevitable Choice for China to Break Through the Bottleneck of Poverty Reduction

At the time of writing, China has launched a new round of poverty alleviation with an accompanying development plan mainly targeting at those experiencing ecological poverty. The main task has shifted from resolving problems of food and clothing to consolidating previous achievements, accelerating efforts to become better off, improving the ecological environment and development ability, and narrowing the development gap in the new stage of national progress. In a sense, the poverty problem plaguing the ecologically vulnerable areas is equal to the ecological problems being experienced, with the occurrence and extent of poverty being closely related to the ecological environment (Liu 2005). Therefore, poverty alleviation in these areas must begin with an effort to improve the ecological environment and enhance regional resources and the local environment carrying capacity, and then coordinate the goals of ecological improvement and poverty reduction, so as to implement an overall ecological poverty reduction strategy.

This refers to a new kind of poverty alleviation mode designed for ecologically poor areas, a new poverty alleviation and development model rooted in the concept of inclusive development. It is geared to ending the vicious cycle of poverty and ecological destruction by protecting and restoring the environment in poverty-stricken areas, transforming the local economic development pattern, and taking into account the goals of ecological improvement and poverty reduction. Given the low participation of local residents seen in previous ecological projects, economic development that is related to ecological protection policies, the fact that the poor hardly benefit from ecological improvements and other issues, and combining with the characteristics of poverty reduction efforts in the current stage, we believe that a successful ecological poverty reduction strategy may contain the following points.

7.4.1 Ecological Improvement as a Fundamental of Poverty Alleviation and the Foundation of Development

Owing to the low carrying capacity of resources and environment, economic and social development in ecologically vulnerable areas encountered a bottleneck. The only way to achieve regional sustainable development, therefore, was to seek a more rational use of resources and improve the ecological environment. Causes of poverty in these areas are diverse, including low income due to inadequate resources access, low capability due to low developmental ability, and lack of rights resulting from persistent inequality of opportunities. The poor bear the brunt of ecological deterioration because it squeezes their living space even further, curtails their access to resources and opportunities, thereby aggravating their poverty. In other words, ecological improvement is the fundamental solution to poverty.

In the absence of sustained ecological improvement, poverty relief through aid and assistance alone can do little more than ensuring subsistence of the poor. It is burdensome to the government over the long term, and a highly inefficient and unsustainable approach to poverty reduction. Development-oriented poverty reduction, however, might be environmentally destructive, leading to a vicious cycle of poverty and ecological destruction. This means that until resource conditions and the environmental carrying capacity of ecologically vulnerable areas are significantly improved, any attempt to alleviate poverty by growing the economy and boosting regional development would be ultimately be futile.

7.4.2 Continuous Ecological Improvement Is Premised on Equal Participation of the Poor

Intuitively speaking, ecological poverty has been a result of population pressure, which gave rise to a continued destruction and then deterioration of the ecological environment. However, a deeper reason is "policy deficiencies", which means the unfair policy excluding those with poor capacity to progress from the development process leading to intensified regional developmental imbalance. Fearing that participation of the poor would affect the results of ecological improvement, local residents were often seen as a burden on the construction of the NFRPP project, wildlife conservation and creation of nature reserves and other large-scale ecological projects, leading to the allocation of subsidies to solve their bread-and-butter issues. However, the poor local population naturally regarded ecological projects as poverty alleviation projects, hence demanded compensation for their economic activity giving way to the proposed construction work. Excluding locals from ecological construction projects increases the cost of construction, and, at the same time, cannot fundamentally reduce the pressure on resources and the environment from activities by the local population for its survival and development. This is due to the lack of inclusiveness in project policies.

Therefore, most importantly, the implementation of ecological poverty reduction strategy should be based on regional resources, including natural and human resources, fully mobilizing all positive factors, and striving to improve the ecological environment and build a solid foundation for the poverty reduction and development of vulnerable areas. In fact, impoverished people have more interest in the projects undertaken to improve the ecological environment where they are the direct victims of ecological deterioration, hence expecting more than other groups in regard to expanding their development space and enhancing development capacity amid continuous ecological improvement. As a result, they constitute the lasting power for regional ecological improvement.

7.4.3 The Ecological Economy Is the Driving Force of Ecological Improvement and Poverty Reduction

Rapid economic growth is a necessary condition for effective poverty reduction, and the key to ecological improvement. Economic development in ecologically vulnerable areas should start from improving the ecological environment, giving priority to the development of the ecological industry. Ecological economy construction is a process in which the economic structure, production method and lifestyle in areas facing ecological poverty are transformed to protect and build the ecological environment in the impoverished areas (Huang 2004). The development of the ecological economy, characterized by indirect undermining of the regional ecological environment and lower dependency on consumption of natural resources, is a sunrise industry suited to the development of ecologically vulnerable areas.

The advantages of ecologically vulnerable areas lie in its featured products and landscape resources. Ecological economy development based on these special resources can promote regional employment. Furthermore, it possesses a competitive advantage capable of attracting foreign investment, becoming a development way giving due consideration to regional economic growth and environmental protection goals. An abundance of eco-industries can be developed in these areas, such as ecological agriculture, agriculture-forestry-husbandry compound management, ecotourism, and so on. which constitute a development model suitable for participation of the poor, seeing quick returns in terms of poverty alleviation and being good for ecological improvement.

7.4.4 The Ecological Compensation Is a Feedback to Sharing the Results of Ecological Improvement

Deterioration of the ecological environment in ecologically vulnerable areas will not only lead to local poverty, but also spread throughout the ecosystem. Under the action of various natural forces (wind, water) and so on, the deteriorated ecological environment will inevitably lead to the destruction and deterioration of the surrounding environment without timely treatment. At present, China's ecological projects are mainly aimed at tackling national or key regional ecological problems, such as the Grain for Green Program, and Beijing-Tianjin region sandstorm abatement project. Ecological improvement of the project area has brought remarkable positive externalities for the surrounding area. Functioning as an ecological barrier, ecologically vulnerable areas should be compensated, as a feedback from the surrounding area in sharing the good ecological services, as well as a support for the ecological management in ecologically vulnerable areas.

Ecological compensation is an economic measure to balance the interests of the relevant subjects of ecological protection, and an important part of the ecological poverty reduction strategy. It enables an ecologically vulnerable zone to directly benefit from ecological protection and improvement. China's ecological compensation mechanism is still in its infancy, mainly involving investment by the central government and giving nominal subsidies to forests, grasslands and wetlands with an important ecological niche. Therefore, ecological compensation can be the key areas for the exploration of ecological poverty reduction strategies. ecologically vulnerable areas may obtain external financial support through the establishment of ecological compensation mechanism at different levels, and better achieve ecological improvement and poverty alleviation objectives.

References

Chen, J. (2008). *Study on rural chronic poverty in ecologically vulnerable areas.* Southwestern University of Finance and Economics.

Huang, S. (2004). Ideas on anti-poverty in rural areas of western ethnic minority areas. *Academic Forum* (4).

Li, Y. (2009). Grain for green program as importantly beneficial for china's ecological civilization construction. *Forestry Construction* (5).

Liu, Y. (2005). Ecological Poverty and Anti-poverty Strategy of Western Areas. *Journal of Harbin Institute of Technology (Social Science Edition)* (6).

Long, C. (2012). Economic growth, people's livelihood construction and inclusive development. *Economist* (3).

Ministry of Environmental Protection. (2008). *Outline for the Conservation of Ecologically Vulnerable Areas in China.*

National Bureau of Statistics. (2010). *Poverty Monitoring Report of Rural China 2010.* China Statistics Press.

State Forestry Administration. (2011). *China Forestry Development Report 2011.* China Forestry Publishing House.

Wang, Y. (1993). Poverty and the environment—breaking the vicious circle, China population. *Resources and Environment* (2).

Wang, Y., & Qiao, Y. (2011). Problems and Solutions in Implementation of Rehabilitating Degraded Grassland with Grazing Ban. *Issues in Agricultural Economy* (2).

Yan, T. (2005). Back to poverty: Pain and embarrassment of anti-poverty. *The World of Survey and Research* (1).

Zhou, L., & Ruomei, S. (1994). Study on correlation of ecologically sensitive areas and poverty-stricken areas. *China Rural Survey* (5).

MIX
Papier aus verantwortungsvollen Quellen
Paper from responsible sources
FSC® C105338

Printed by Books on Demand, Germany